ON TRACK

Video Activity Book

Susan Parks

Gerard Bates

Anna Thibeault

Mary Lee Wholey

Oxford University Press

Oxford University Press
Walton Street, Oxford OX2 6DP

Oxford   New York
Athens   Auckland   Bangkok   Bombay
Calcutta   Cape Town   Dar es Salaam   Delhi
Florence   Hong Kong   Istanbul   Karachi
Kuala Lumpur   Madras   Madrid   Melbourne
Mexico City   Nairobi   Paris   Singapore
Taipei   Tokyo   Toronto

and associated companies in
Berlin   Ibadan

Oxford and Oxford English are trade marks
of Oxford University Press

First published 1990
Fourth impression 1994

ISBN 0 19 458496 8 (Video Activity Book)
ISBN 0 19 458497 6 (Video Guide)

ISBN 0 19 458498 4 (VHS PAL Video Cassette)
ISBN 0 19 458499 2 (VHS SECAM Video Cassette)
ISBN 0 19 458500 X (VHS NTSC Video Cassette)
ISBN 0 19 458501 8 (BETAMAX PAL Video Cassette)
ISBN 0 19 458502 6 (BETAMAX SECAM Video Cassette)
ISBN 0 19 458503 4 (BETAMAX NTSC Video Cassette)

Illustrations by
JENNY HILL
JANE HUGHES
JIM ROBINS
ALEX McOWAN

*The Publishers would like to thank the following for their
permission to reproduce photographs:*
IMAGE BANK *(cover photograph)*
GREG EVANS PHOTO LIBRARY *(page 30)*

Printed in Hong Kong

Acknowledgement

Special thanks are extended to Dr Douglas J Potvin, former
Director of the Centre for Continuing Education, Concordia
University, Montreal, and the staff of the Centre for
Continuing Education for their support in the publication of
this material.

Video Credits

Executive Producers
DR DOUGLAS POTVIN
MARK SCHOFIELD

Producer/Director
MICHAEL KEEFFE

Director of Photography
RODNEY GIBBONS

Technical Director
MICHAEL McGEE

Camera Operators
KEITH YOUNG
STEPHEN CAMPANELLI

Sound Operator
RICHARD NICHOL

Electrician
WALTER KLYMKIW

Best Boy
DAVID SETTER
BRIAN BAKER

Key Grip
J F BOURASSA

Scriptwriters
GERARD BATES
SUSAN PARKS
ANNA THIBEAULT
MARY LEE WHOLEY

Script Consultant
ERNA BUFFIE

ESL Project Co-ordinator
SUSAN PARKS

Production Manager
DEBRA d'ENTREMONT

Assistant Director
DON TERRY

Set Designs and Props
ANDREW CAMPBELL
MARIANNE SZABO

Make-Up
ANDRE MORNEAU
TOM BOOTH

Wardrobe
SYLVIE OUAKNINE

Production Assistants
MARIE JOSEE MARCIL
JEAN PAUL REMILLIEUX
VIDAR NEUHOF

Production Secretaries
CLARA PARADISIS
LUISA FRAZZETTO
ELIZABETH RUSZKOWSKI

Off-Line Editors
PETER BLYSZCZAK
DEBRA d'ENTREMONT
MICHAEL KEEFFE

On-Line Editor
RICARDO FUOCO

Assistant Editor
FABRICE PETIT

Post-Production Audio
PIERRE L'ABBE

Computer Graphic 2D
MARIE DIONNE

Title Music
BRENT HOLLAND

On-Line Facility
ONZIEME CIEL

with special thanks to:
LUIGI IAMMATTEO
DANIEL CLAVEAU
of ONZIEME CIEL

*Technical Operations and
Research and Development*
AUDIO-VISUAL DEPARTMENT
CONCORDIA UNIVERSITY

Produced by
THE CENTRE FOR
CONTINUING EDUCATION &
AUDIO-VISUAL DEPARTMENT
CONCORDIA UNIVERSITY,
MONTREAL

Contents

1 The customer is always right

CHRISTA

A Blouse. 100% silk.
White or grey.
Small, medium, large.
SAVE $22.
Regular price $99
Sale price $77

B Belt.
Red or black leather.
$80

C Skirt. 100% cotton.
Red or green.
Sizes 8 to 14.
$125

Look at the pictures. Answer these questions about Christa.

What is Christa wearing?

Does the skirt come in red?

Does the skirt also come in brown?

Does the skirt come in size 10?

How much does the skirt cost? The blouse? The belt?

Which is more expensive – the skirt or the blouse?

Is the blouse on sale? How much can you save?

What is the skirt made of? The blouse? The belt?

DAVE   JULIE   CARLOS   JACKIE

A • Jacket.
100% cotton.
White or black.
Sizes small,
medium, large,
or extra large.
Only $29.99

B • Pants.
100% cotton.
White, black, or brown.
Sizes 30 to 42.
Only $19.99

C • Shirt. 100% cotton.
White, yellow, or pink.
Small, medium or large.
SAVE $5.00
Regular price $15.00
Sale price $10.00

A • Scarf. 100% silk.
Pink, green or blue.
$25.99

B • Dress. 100% cotton.
Yellow or green.
Sizes 8 to 14.
$169

C • Bag.
Brown or black leather.
$75.45

A • Sweater. 100% wool.
Blue or red.
Small, medium or large.
$50

B • Pants. 100% cotton.
Black or brown.
Sizes 30 to 44.
SAVE $10
Regular price $75
Sale price $65

A • Coat. 100% cotton.
Pink or grey.
Sizes 10 to 14.
Only $85

B • Bag.
White or black leather.
SAVE $10
Regular price $50
Sale price $40

◖◗ *Ask and answer questions about Julie and Dave in pairs.*

Is Julie wearing a skirt or a dress?

What sizes does it come in?

How much does it cost?

Which is more expensive – Julie's dress or Christa's skirt?

What is Julie carrying over her shoulder?

What does she have around her neck?

What is Dave wearing?

What colors does the jacket come in?

What is the shirt made of?

Is it on sale? If yes, how much can you save?

◖◗ *Now in your pairs, ask and answer questions about Jackie and Carlos.*

Activity 1

Here are the main characters in the video.

The Customer   The Salesclerk

Read the questions. Then watch the video and try to get the answers.

What does the customer want to buy?
Do the customer and the salesclerk like the same things?
Does the customer buy any clothes?

 Watch the video. (00:00 – 05:58)

Activity 2

 Read through these statements and in groups decide if they are true or false.
Put a check mark ✓ in the box. If the answer is 'False', give the correct information.

		True	False
1	The customer is shopping for shoes.	☐	☐
2	The salesclerk takes the customer's coat and bag.	☐	☐
3	The customer is well-dressed.	☐	☐
4	The customer says she takes size 12.	☐	☐
5	The new winter color is pink.	☐	☐
6	The blue dress has a belt.	☐	☐
7	The blue dress is this year's style.	☐	☐
8	The customer wants a brown skirt.	☐	☐
9	The customer likes the skirt with the design.	☐	☐
10	The customer doesn't like the green skirt.	☐	☐
11	The shoulders of the pink dress are too tight.	☐	☐
12	The salesclerk likes the grey blouse.	☐	☐
13	The black suit costs $150.00	☐	☐
14	The red suit is more expensive than the black suit.	☐	☐
15	The customer doesn't try on the black suit.	☐	☐
16	The black suit is the latest style.	☐	☐
17	The customer buys the pink dress and the black suit.	☐	☐

 Now watch the video and check your answers. (00:00 – 05:58)

After you watch, discuss your answers in your group.

4

Activity 3

Watch the video and answer your teacher's questions. (00:00 – 01:00)

Activity 4

Complete the conversation with the words from the list.

beautiful
pink
blue (2)
certainly
style (2)
dress
belt
color (2)
nice
both

Salesclerk: This is our latest _ _ _ _ _ _ . Isn't it _ _ _ _ _ _ ?
Customer: I don't really like the _ _ _ _ _ _ . Do you have something in _ _ _ _ _ _ ?
Salesclerk: No. This _ _ _ _ _ _ only comes in _ _ _ _ _ _ . Pink is the new winter _ _ _ _ _ _ .
Customer: Here's one in _ _ _ _ _ _ . I love the _ _ _ _ _ _ .
Salesclerk: Yes, it's _ _ _ _ _ _ , but it is last year's _ _ _ _ _ _ .
Customer: Maybe, I can try them _ _ _ _ _ _ on.
Salesclerk: _ _ _ _ _ _ , madam.
Customer: Thank you.

Discuss your answers with a partner.

Now watch the video and check your answers. (01:05 – 01:32)

Activity 5

Watch the video and answer your teacher's questions. (01:33 – 02:07)

Activity 6

Watch this part of the video twice and fill in the missing words. (02:08 – 03:17)

Customer: Hey, just a minute, please. I'd like to _ _ _ _ _ _ one of these _ _ _ _ _ _ . I like this _ _ _ _ _ _ . It's only _ _ _ _ _ _ dollars. You _ _ _ _ _ _ ?
Salesclerk: I think you'd look much better in _ _ _ _ _ _ .
Customer: How much _ _ _ _ _ _ ?
Salesclerk: It was _ _ _ _ _ _ , but it's been reduced to _ _ _ _ _ _ .
Customer: _ _ _ _ _ _ is a lot of money! It's _ _ _ _ _ _ than this one.
Salesclerk: Believe me, madam, it's worth the extra _ _ _ _ _ _ . Just look at _ _ _ _ _ _ and _ _ _ _ _ _ .
Customer: Well, maybe I could . . .
Salesclerk: _ _ _ _ _ _ both on? Yes, _ _ _ _ _ _ . Would you like a blouse?
Customer: What _ _ _ _ _ _ ?
Salesclerk: Follow me, please.

Discuss your answers with a partner.

Activity 7

Complete the conversation with the words from the list.

beautiful	like	try on (2)
last	comfortable	shoulders
scarf	long	dress
wear	wonderful	shorten
buy		

Customer: I love it. It's so _ _ _ _ _ _ . You don't _ _ _ _ _ _ it.
Salesclerk: Well, it is _ _ _ _ _ _ year's style. Why don't you _ _ _ _ _ _ the pink one I showed you?

(The customer tries on the pink dress.)

Salesclerk: _ _ _ _ _ _ ! It's _ _ _ _ _ _ on you.
Customer: Yes, but the _ _ _ _ _ _ are too tight, and it's too _ _ _ _ _ _ .
Salesclerk: Well, we can _ _ _ _ _ _ it. Or you can _ _ _ _ _ _ it with a belt. And this _ _ _ _ _ _ is perfect! . . . You do like the _ _ _ _ _ _ , don't you?
Customer: Yes . . .
Salesclerk: Well, then I think you should _ _ _ _ _ _ it. Now, why don't you _ _ _ _ _ _ the skirts?

Discuss your answers with a partner.

Now watch the video and check your answers. (03:20 – 04:19)

Activity 8

Watch the video and answer your teacher's questions. (04:20 – 04:39)

Activity 9

Complete the conversation with words from the list.

try on	latest	nice	decision (2)
right	good	a lot of	suit
looked	take it in		

Customer: Now, this looks _ _ _ _ _ _ , doesn't it?
Salesclerk: Yes, it's _ _ _ _ _ _ , but the color . . .
Customer: I thought I _ _ _ _ _ _ good in red.
Salesclerk: Well, it's up to you, but I really think that you should . . .
Customer: _ _ _ _ _ _ the black _ _ _ _ _ _ !

(The customer tries on the black suit.)

Customer: It's too big.
Salesclerk: We can _ _ _ _ _ _ .
Customer: Three hundred and fifty dollars is _ _ _ _ _ _ money.
Salesclerk: It is the _ _ _ _ _ _ style.
Customer: I know that, but . . .
Salesclerk: Well, it is your _ _ _ _ _ _ .
Customer: You're _ _ _ _ _ _ . It is my _ _ _ _ _ _ .

Discuss your answers with a partner.

Now watch the video and check your answers. (04:40 – 05:24)

Activity 1

WHO SAID THIS?

Write S for Salesclerk and C for Customer.

S	May I take your coat and bag?
	That's right. I'm looking for a dress.
	What size do you take?
	I think a size 12 would fit you perfectly.
	This is beautiful. Does it come in brown?
	You can try them both on.
	How much does it cost?
	Well, it is last year's style.
	Well, it is your decision.
	No, I won't regret it.

Discuss your answers with a partner.

Activity 2

WHICH LINE COMES NEXT?

Match the sentences in Column A with the replies in Column B.

COLUMN A	COLUMN B
May I help you with anything?	No. This dress only comes in pink.
Would you like to look at the skirts?	Yes. It's nice, but the color . . .
Now, this looks good, doesn't it?	$350.00.
Do you have something in blue?	What size do you take?
How much does it cost?	Not right now, thank you. I'm just looking.
I'm looking for a dress.	Well, we can shorten it.
But the shoulders are too tight, and it's too long.	Sure. What do you have?

Discuss your answers with a partner.

Activity 3

ROLE PLAY

Read through the script silently. Then read out the script in pairs. The script is on page 58. Now role-play the story.

Follow up

LANGUAGE CHECK

Activity 1

Complete the conversation.

Salesclerk: Hello. _ _ _ _ _ _ I help you?
Customer: Yes, I'm looking for a skirt.
Salesclerk: _ _ _ _ _ _ do you take?
Customer: Size 12.
Salesclerk: _ _ _ _ _ _ do you want?
Customer: Blue.
Salesclerk: Fine. Here's one in blue.
Customer: _ _ _ _ _ _ does it cost?
Salesclerk: $75.
Customer: OK. _ _ _ _ _ _ I try it on?
Salesclerk: Sure. Follow me.
Customer: Oh, I like this red skirt, too.
Salesclerk: Well, _ _ _ _ _ _ don't you try them both on?
Customer: OK.

Discuss your answers with a partner.

Activity 2

Complete the conversation using the Simple Present.

Customer: I'm looking for a shirt.
Salesclerk: What size _ _ _ _ _ _ (take)?
Customer: Medium.
Salesclerk: Here _ _ _ _ _ _ (be) a nice one. _ _ _ _ _ _ (like) it?
Customer: No, I _ _ _ _ _ _ (not, like) the style.
Salesclerk: Well, how about this one?
Customer: Yes, but _ _ _ _ _ _ (come) in green?
Salesclerk: Yes. Here _ _ _ _ _ _ (be) a green one.
Customer: How much _ _ _ _ _ _ (cost)?
Salesclerk: It only _ _ _ _ _ _ (cost) $22. It _ _ _ _ _ _ (be) on sale.
Customer: Good. Oh, it also _ _ _ _ _ _ (come) in brown. I _ _ _ _ _ _ (like) that one too.
Salesclerk: Well, why _ _ _ _ _ _ (not, buy) them both?
Customer: OK.

Discuss your answers with a partner.

READING RETELL

Read Text A and answer the questions.

1 Who is Charles Martin?

2 What does he design?

3 Where does he live?

4 Does he live alone?

5 What does he do in his free time?

6 Where does he like to go on vacation?

7 When did he come to Canada?

8 When did he start working in a clothing store?

9 What did he sell at school?

10 Where did he keep the jeans?

11 Why did he travel to Paris?

12 What did he do when he returned to Montreal?

13 Why did he sell his stores?

14 Where can you buy his clothes?

◼◉ **Check your answers with a partner.**

Retell your story to a student with Text B.

TEXT A

Charles Martin: A Fashion Designer

Charles Martin is a famous fashion designer. He designs jeans, jackets, skirts and dresses. Charles works very hard. He often works twelve hours a day and sometimes on weekends too. His company is in Montreal, but he lives on a farm outside the city. He lives there with his parents and three brothers. In his free time, he likes to go horseback riding. He also has a black belt in karate and enjoys this sport very much. He likes to travel. When he takes a vacation, he likes to go to a place with hot, sunny weather and nice beaches.

Charles came to Canada from France when he was five years old. At fifteen, he started working in a clothing store. At school, he made money by selling jeans to other students. He kept the jeans in his locker. He sold a lot of jeans. Some weeks he made more money than his teachers. After he finished school, he travelled to Paris to study fashion design. When he returned to Montreal, he opened his own clothing store. At age 23, he had four stores. But he wanted to spend all his time designing clothes so he sold his stores. Today, you can buy his clothes in stores in Canada, the United States and Europe. Charles is very successful and very rich.

Read Text B and answer the questions.

1 What is Tracey's job?

2 When Tracey was a little girl, did she think she was pretty?

3 When did she begin to play basketball?

4 Was she the best player on her team?

5 Who saw Tracey when she was sixteen?

6 What did he ask Tracey to do?

7 Is modeling easy or hard?

8 When does Tracey's work day begin?

9 Does Tracey always work inside?

10 When does she get home?

11 Where does she travel to?

12 How many sisters does she have?

13 Does Tracey fight with her sisters?

14 Does Tracey want to continue modeling?

15 What does Tracey want to study at university?

◨● **Check your answers with a partner.**

Retell your story to a student with Text A.

TEXT B

Tracey Wilkinson: A Fashion Model

Tracey Wilkinson is only sixteen but she has an exciting job. She is a fashion model. Tracey didn't plan to be a fashion model. When she was a little girl, she didn't think that she was very pretty. She thought that her feet were too big. She always tried to hide her feet under her school desk. She was also very tall. She was the tallest person in her class. When Tracey was fourteen, she began to play basketball. Soon she was the best player on her team. One day, a fashion photographer saw her playing basketball. He asked her to model for a popular sports magazine. Her picture was on the cover and soon she was famous.

People think that modeling is easy but it's not. When she models, Tracey works hard. Her work day begins very early. Sometimes she works inside under hot lights all day. Sometimes she works for many hours outside in the cold. She often gets home very late at night. She travels a lot. One week she is in New York and the next week she is in London and Paris. But when Tracey is at home she is just an ordinary girl. She has two younger sisters. She likes her sisters but sometimes they fight. She likes to listen to rock music and go to horror movies with her friends. Tracey doesn't want to continue modeling for many years. When she finishes school, she wants to study medicine at university.

Functions

Now you can:

Offer/Accept/Refuse help	May I help you? Thank you very much. No, not right now, I'm just looking. May I take your coat and bag? Would you like a blouse?
Express likes	I like the buttons. I love the belt.
Express dislikes	I don't really like the color.
Ask for information	What size do you take? How much does it cost? Do you have this in blue?
Express dissatisfaction	It's too long/big.
Express agreement	That's right. Certainly.
Make a suggestion	Why don't you try on the pink one?

Structures

Present simple 'to be'	I am a little warm in this. Pink is the new winter color. You are here to buy new clothes.
Present simple	This dress only comes in pink. I like this one.
Negative:	I don't really like the color.
Interrogative:	Do you have something in blue? Does it come in brown?
Imperative	Follow me, please. Wait.
Question words	What size do you take? What do you have? Why don't you try on the pink one? How much does it cost?
'too' + adjective	It's too long. The shoulders are too tight.
'this'/'that'	This is a size 12. That is a size 8. I like this one in green.

Words and expressions

clothes	to buy	size	big	It's up to you!
coat	to wear	style	small	Wonderful!
bag	to fit	material	long	Sure!
dress	to try on	design	short	Certainly.
suit	to take in		tight	That's right.
skirt	to shorten	blue	nice	Follow me, please.
blouse	to help	pink	comfortable	I'm just looking.
belt	to look for	brown	perfect	Here's one in blue.
scarf	to regret	black	lovely	Hey, just a minute!
buttons		red		Yes, of course.
		green		

Doctor knows best

Look at the questionnaire. Answer these questions about yourself. Then ask the questions to three students. Write the answers on the questionnaire form.

	Your name	Student A	Student B	Student C
1 Do you drink coffee? If yes, how many cups a day?				
2 Do you smoke cigarettes? If yes, how many do you smoke a day?				
3 Do you eat junk food (hot dogs, French fries, chocolate bars)?				
4 Do you work/study? If yes, how many hours a day?				
5 What do you do to relax?				
6 How many hours do you sleep at night?				

Find out about the class. Ask these questions to your group.

Who drinks the most coffee?

Who smokes the most cigarettes?

Who eats junk food? What kind?

Who works/studies the most hours a day?

What do people in your group do to relax?

Who sleeps the most at night?

Activity 1

Here are the main characters in the video.

| Mr Hunter | Doctor Pachesky | The Receptionist |

Read the questions. Then watch the video and try to get the answers.

Why does Mr. Hunter go to see the doctor?
What does the doctor tell Mr. Hunter to stop doing?
What does Mr. Hunter tell the doctor to stop doing?

 Watch the video. (06:18 – 13:48)

Activity 2

 *Read through these statements and in groups decide if they are true or false.
Put a check mark in the box. If the answer is 'False', give the correct information.*

	True	False
1 You can smoke in the doctor's office.	☐	☐
2 Mr. Hunter tries to hide his cigarette.	☐	☐
3 Mr. Hunter waited for the doctor for an hour and a half.	☐	☐
4 Mr. Hunter is worried about his heart.	☐	☐
5 Mr. Hunter is thirty years old.	☐	☐
6 Mr. Hunter only smokes one pack of cigarettes a day.	☐	☐
7 Mr. Hunter drinks eight or nine cups of coffee a day.	☐	☐
8 Coffee is good for the heart.	☐	☐
9 Mr. Hunter works long hours.	☐	☐
10 The doctor checks Mr. Hunter's lungs.	☐	☐
11 The doctor doesn't order any tests for Mr. Hunter.	☐	☐
12 The doctor tells Mr. Hunter to quit smoking.	☐	☐
13 Mr. Hunter makes another appointment.	☐	☐
14 The doctor asks the receptionist for fruit juice.	☐	☐
15 Mr. Hunter is surprised to see that the doctor smokes.	☐	☐
16 The doctor doesn't drink coffee.	☐	☐
17 The receptionist thinks the doctor should stop smoking.	☐	☐
18 The doctor keeps his pack of cigarettes.	☐	☐

 Now watch the video and check your answers. (06:18 – 13:49)

After you watch, discuss your answers in your group.

Activity 3

Watch the video and answer your teacher's questions.(06:18 – 08:22)

Activity 4

Complete the conversation with the words from the list.

yesterday	hurt
describe	rest
turned	dizzy
worried	heart
pain	sharp
breathe	work

Doctor: So, what can I do for you today?
Mr. Hunter: Well, I'm a little _ _ _ _ _ _ about my _ _ _ _ _ _ .
Doctor: Oh really? Well, why are you so worried?
Mr. Hunter: _ _ _ _ _ _ , when I was at _ _ _ _ _ _ I got a _ _ _ _ _ _ , ah . . . right here.
Doctor: Could you _ _ _ _ _ _ it to me?
Mr. Hunter: Well, it started out as a dull ache and then it _ _ _ _ _ _ into a _ _ _ _ _ _ pain. It really _ _ _ _ _ _ .
Doctor: Anything else?
Mr. Hunter: Yeah, I felt _ _ _ _ _ _ and I could hardly _ _ _ _ _ _ . I had to sit down and _ _ _ _ _ _ for fifteen minutes.

Discuss your answers with a partner.

Now watch the video and check your answers. (08:52 – 09:27)

Activity 5

Complete the conversation with words from the list.

long	coffee	know
drink (2)	cups	health
relaxes	like	years

Doctor: Do you smoke?
Mr. Hunter: Yeah.
Doctor: How much?
Mr. Hunter: A pack a day . . . sometimes two.
Doctor: How long have you been smoking?
Mr. Hunter: Oh, I don't _ _ _ _ _ _ . Twenty _ _ _ _ _ _ , maybe longer.
Doctor: Twenty years is a _ _ _ _ _ _ time, a long time.
Mr. Hunter: I know. But I _ _ _ _ _ _ to smoke. It _ _ _ _ _ _ me.
Doctor: Oh, I understand. I understand. But it's bad for your _ _ _ _ _ _ . Do you _ _ _ _ _ _ a lot of _ _ _ _ _ _ too?
Mr. Hunter: Yeah, but I've cut down a lot lately.
Doctor: How many _ _ _ _ _ _ a day?
Mr. Hunter: Oh, . . . eight or nine.
Doctor: Two or three cups a day is all you should _ _ _ _ _ _ . It's bad for the heart.

Discuss your answers with a partner.

Now watch the video and check your answers. (09:40 – 10:26)

Activity 6

Watch the video and answer your teacher's questions. (10:34 – 11:18)

Activity 7

Watch this part of the video twice and fill in the missing words. (12:39 – 13:20)

Doctor: Julie, do we have any fresh _ _ _ _ _ _ ? Mr. Hunter! You're still here?

Mr. Hunter: You _ _ _ _ _ _ !

Doctor: What? Oh this! Well . . . well you're a _ _ _ _ _ _ . You _ _ _ _ _ _ how it is, Mr. Hunter. You smoke.

Mr. Hunter: Not anymore. I just _ _ _ _ _ _ . How many _ _ _ _ _ _ does he drink?

Receptionist: About _ _ _ _ _ _ a day.

Mr. Hunter: Ten cups! Doesn't he know that _ _ _ _ _ _ for _ _ _ _ _ _ .

Doctor: Ah, but I _ _ _ _ _ _ long hours. I _ _ _ _ _ _ coffee.

Mr. Hunter: And that cough! I really think he _ _ _ _ _ _ , don't you?

Discuss your answers with a partner.

Activity 1

WHO SAID THIS?

Write R for receptionist, H for Mr. Hunter and D for the doctor.

	Do you have an ashtray?
	No, Mr. Hunter I don't smoke.
	The doctor will see you now.
	Oh, its only been about a half an hour.
	I'm a little worried about my heart.
	Could you describe it to me?
	Two or three cups a day is all you should drink.
	All right, we're just going to check your lungs.
	Doesn't he know that that's bad for his heart?
	The whole pack, please.

Discuss your answers with a partner.

Activity 2

WHICH LINE COMES NEXT?

Match the sentences in Column A with the replies in Column B.

COLUMN A	COLUMN B
Do you have an ashtray?	That's OK.
Sorry to keep you waiting.	About 45.
Do you think it's my heart?	Yes. I'm surprised. It's excellent.
How old are you?	Right. Thanks a lot.
Is it OK?	No, I don't smoke.
Then there is something wrong.	I'm not sure.
If there's anything you need, just call.	You smoke!
Mr. Hunter! You're still here?	About ten cups a day.
How many cups a day does he drink?	There's nothing to worry about.

Discuss your answers with a partner.

Activity 3

ROLE PLAY

Read through the script silently. Then get into groups of three and read out the script. The script is on page 58. Now role-play the story.

LANGUAGE CHECK

Activity 1

Fill in the blanks with the correct form of the verb using the Present tense.

Dr. Pachesky works very hard - maybe too hard. At 6:00 he _ _ _ _ _ _ (get up) and gets dressed for work. _ _ _ _ _ _ he _ _ _ _ _ _ (eat) breakfast? No. He _ _ _ _ _ _ (have) a cup of coffee and a cigarette. He _ _ _ _ _ _ (leave) his house at 6:30 and _ _ _ _ _ _ (go) to the hospital. He _ _ _ _ _ _ (be) a busy man. He _ _ _ _ _ _ (examine) ten to fifteen different patients. He _ _ _ _ _ _ (work) all morning. He _ _ _ _ _ _ (not, stop). He _ _ _ _ _ _ (smoke) more cigarettes and _ _ _ _ _ _ (drink) more coffee. He _ _ _ _ _ _ (not relax) at work. At 12:00 he _ _ _ _ _ _ (eat) lunch. What _ _ _ _ _ _ he _ _ _ _ _ _ (eat)? He _ _ _ _ _ _ (not, have) much time, so he _ _ _ _ _ _ (order) a hot dog and a soft drink. Then he _ _ _ _ _ _ (drive) to his office and _ _ _ _ _ _ (see) more patients. He usually _ _ _ _ _ _ (finish) at 6:30. He never _ _ _ _ _ _ (stop) before 6:00. _ _ _ _ _ _ he _ _ _ _ _ _ (relax) at home? Rarely. People _ _ _ _ _ _ (telephone) the doctor at home, and he often _ _ _ _ _ _ (return) to the hospital when there _ _ _ _ _ _ (be) an emergency.

Discuss your answers with a partner.

Activity 2

Complete the following conversations.

Patient: Hello. I'd like to make an appointment.
Receptionist: Yes, what time _ _ _ _ _ _ like?
Patient: I'm free tomorrow at 4:30.
Receptionist: Good, we'll _ _ _ _ _ _ you tomorrow at 4:30.

Doctor: _ _ _ _ _ _ can I do for you today?
Patient: Well, I'm worried about my cough.
Doctor: _ _ _ _ _ _ are you so worried?
Patient: Well because yesterday, at work, I couldn't stop coughing.

Doctor: _ _ _ _ _ _ coffee do you drink?
Patient: Eight or nine cups a day.
Doctor: That's _ _ _ _ _ _ much.
Patient: _ _ _ _ _ _ cups can I drink?
Doctor: Two or three cups is all you should drink.

Patient Doctor, I _ _ _ _ _ _ terrible!
Doctor: What's the matter?
Patient: I have a headache.
Doctor: Can you _ _ _ _ _ _ it?
Patient: Yes, it's a sharp pain and then it turns into a dull ache.

Discuss your answers with a partner.

READING RETELL

Read Text A and answer the questions.

1 What is Leonard O'Connor's job?

2 What will he do tomorrow?

3 What is he doing now?

4 How many children does Mary Wilson have?

5 What does Dr. O'Connor tell Mary?

6 What time does Dr. O'Connor go to bed?

7 What is he thinking about?

8 When does he get up?

9 Why does he dress quietly?

10 What does he do at his office?

11 Does he always listen to music before an operation?

12 When is he ready to operate?

13 When does he begin the most difficult part of the operation?

14 How long does the operation take?

15 Is the operation a success?

📢 **Check your answers with a partner.**

Retell your story to a student with Text B.

TEXT A

A Difficult Operation

Leonard O'Connor is a doctor. He is one of the best brain surgeons in the world. It is Sunday evening. Dr. O'Connor is at the hospital. He is talking to his patient, Mary Wilson. He will operate on her tomorrow. It is a dangerous operation. Mary's husband and three children are with her at the hospital. She is very nervous but Dr. O'Connor tells her not to worry. He is optimistic. Mary feels better after she talks to the doctor. Then, Dr. O'Connor goes home. At 10:30 p.m. he goes to bed but he can't sleep. He is thinking about the operation tomorrow. He's thinking about what he will do and how he will do it.

It is Monday 6:05 a.m.. Dr. O'Connor gets up and gets dressed quickly. He is very quiet. He doesn't want to wake his wife. At 6:30 he is in his office. He studies Mary's medical records. At 6:50 he turns on his cassette recorder. He listens to music. Music helps him to relax. He always listens to music before an operation.

At 7:22 a.m. he is ready to operate. At 7:30 the operation begins. It is a long operation - twelve hours. At about 4:00 p.m. Dr. O'Connor begins the most difficult part of the operation. He is tired but there is still a lot to do. He must not make any mistakes. At 7:30 p.m. he finishes, after twelve long hours. The operation is a success. Dr. O'Connor is very happy and so is Mary's family.

Read Text B and answer the questions.

1 How many heart attacks did Jack have?

2 What did Jack have to have?

3 How old is Jack?

4 How many children does he have?

5 When did Jack have a heart transplant?

6 Was it successful?

7 How much exercise does Jack do?

8 When does the doctor come to see Jack?

9 What does the doctor do?

10 Can Jack go back to work?

11 How many meals a day can Jack eat?

12 What sports can't Jack play?

13 What does Jack have to quit?

14 Who comes to take Jack home?

15 Who is driving home?

🔲⬤ *Check your answers with a partner.*

Retell your story to a student with Text A.

TEXT B

A New Heart

Jack Clay was a very sick man. He had three heart attacks. His heart stopped completely three times. He almost died. His doctors told him that without a new heart he was going to die soon. A heart transplant was his one hope. Jack thought "I'm only 41 years old. I have a wife and three children. I'm too young to die."

So, one month ago Jack had a heart transplant. It was a success and now he is ready to go home. It is Monday 9:00 a.m.. Jack is beginning his hospital routine for the last time. He does one hour of exercise. He gets on an exercise bicycle and rides for 20 kilometres. He feels very good. At 10:00 a.m. the doctor comes to see Jack. He checks Jack's heart. The new heart is working well. The doctor tells Jack that he can go back to work. He can eat three meals a day, or more if he is hungry. He can exercise but he can't play sports like American football or soccer. The most important thing is he cannot smoke. He has to quit. Jack says, "I smoke three packs a day. It will be hard but I'm going to try. If I don't stop smoking, I won't live very long."

At 11:30 a.m. Jack is ready to go home. He packs his bags. His wife comes to take him home. It's time to say good-bye to the doctors and nurses. Everyone is happy that he is going home. A nurse asks him, "Is your wife driving?" "No", says Jack, "my wife drove here this morning and I am driving back." Jack is beginning his life again with a new heart.

Functions

Now you can:

Introduce yourself	I'm John Hunter.
Make requests	Do you have an ashtray? Could you describe it to me? Would you take off your shirt, please? I would like to ask you a few more questions.
Ask for and give information	How old are you? I'm forty. Do you drink a lot of coffee? About eight or nine cups. Do you smoke? Yes.
Agree with someone	You're right. I know. I understand.
Give advice	It's bad for your health. Coffee's bad for your heart. Two or three cups is all you should drink.

Structures

Present simple 'to be'	I'm John Hunter. I'm not sure. This is a no-smoking area. You're a smoker.
Present simple	I have an appointment. I work long hours. It relaxes me.
Negative:	I don't smoke.
Interrogative:	Do you have an ashtray? How many cups of coffee does he drink?
Future with 'going to'	I'm going to check your lungs. This isn't going to hurt. I'm going to order a few tests. I'm going to quit.
Future with 'will'	I'll need your medical insurance card. We'll see you tomorrow at 4:30. I'll be happy to help.
Imperative	Follow me. Make another appointment. Breathe in/out.
Question words	What can I do for you? How old are you? How much do you smoke? How many cups of coffee does he drink?

Words and expressions

appointment	coffee	to feel	to call (phone)	Excuse me . . .
health	cigarettes	to breathe in/out		Alright.
medical insurance	pack of cigarettes	to hurt	good	OK. You're right.
card	ashtray	to quit (smoking)	bad	I'm worried about . . .
examining table	garbage	to cut down	dull	I'm not sure.
tests		to drink	sharp	. . . maybe (longer)
heart	to ask	to smoke	excellent	(Two cups) a day
lungs	to help	to relax	dizzy	I'll be happy to help.
pain	to need	to rest		
ache	to examine	to worry about	That's great.	
cough	to check	to make (an appointment)	That's OK.	

3 Cooking with Arlene

Spaghetti Sauce

Ingredients

3 or 4 kilos of tomatoes
1 onion
2 green peppers
½ kilo of hamburger
salt
pepper
parsley
oil

Method

1 Put tomatoes into a large saucepan.
2 Pour boiling water over tomatoes.
3 Cook tomatoes on low heat for 1 hour.
4 Chop onions and green pepper.
5 Put oil into frying pan on medium heat.
6 Fry hamburger.
7 Add onions and green pepper to meat.
8 Add meat and vegetables to tomatoes.
9 Add salt, pepper and parsley.
10 Cook for ½ hour on a low heat.

Look at the recipe above and circle the ingredients you need to make spaghetti sauce.

tomatoes   onions   butter   peppers

potatoes   eggs   oil   hamburger   milk

peas   parsley   chicken   carrots

Ask and answer questions about the ingredients needed to make spaghetti sauce.

FOLLOW THE RECIPE

Match the sentences to the correct picture.

1 Pour the boiling water over the tomatoes.
2 Chop the onion.
3 Pour the oil in the pan.
4 Fry the meat in the pan.
5 Add the vegetables to the meat.

🔲 *Discuss your answers with a partner.*

THE KITCHEN

Look at the picture and match the answers with these questions.

1 Where is the bowl of eggs?   ☐ On the stove.
2 Where is the frying pan?   ☐ Beside the counter.
3 Where is the electric beater?   ☐ In the fridge.
4 Where is the fridge?   ☐ Under the carton of milk.
5 Where is the carton of milk?   ☐ Behind the measuring cup.

🔲 *Discuss your answers with a partner.*

Activity 1

Here are the main characters in the video.

Dennis   Janet

Read the questions. Then watch the video and try to get the answers.

Who is doing the cooking show today?
What is today's recipe?
Who is going to do the next show?

Watch the video. (14:18 – 23:10)

Activity 2

Read through these statements and in groups decide if they are true or false.
Put a check mark in the box. If the answer is 'False', give the correct information.

	True	False
1 Arlene is at home.		
2 The boss tells Dennis that he should do the show.	☒	
3 Dennis is happy to do the show.		☒
4 The recipe is for Spanish omelet.		
5 Dennis drops three eggs.		
6 Omelets are difficult to make.		☒
7 Dennis uses an electric beater.	☒	
8 Dennis needs an onion, a green pepper, a tomato, salt and pepper, and some cooking oil.	☒	
9 The onions make Dennis cry.		
10 Dennis likes to sing when he cooks.		
11 Dennis cooks the onion, green pepper and tomato for three minutes.		☒
12 Dennis has to hurry to finish the omelet.		☒
13 Dennis makes a very good omelet.		☒
14 Dennis is happy the show is over.		☒
15 Dennis wants to do more shows.		☒

Now watch the video and check your answers. (14:18 – 23:10)

After you watch, discuss your answers in your group.

Activity 3

Watch the video and answer your teacher's questions. (14:18 – 15:22)

Activity 4

Complete the conversation with words from the list.

recipe	what	cook
omelets	today	Spanish omelets
name	love	

Dennis: My name is Dennis Johnson, so today we'll be "Cooking with Dennis". My _name_ is Dennis.
Janet: The _recipe_!
Dennis: OK . . . So, well, we're here to cook, so let's _ _ _ _ _ _, huh? _ _ _ _ _ _ are we cooking, Janet?
Janet: Spanish _omelet_.
Dennis: Did you hear that, folks? _recipe_ we're cooking _today_. I _love_ omelets, don't you?

Discuss your answers with a partner.

Now watch the video and check your answers. (16:22 – 16:51)

Activity 5

Watch this part of the video twice and fill in the missing words. (17:15 – 18:21)

Dennis: Now then, we have our _eggs_ and the _recipe_ calls for _eggs_ . . . one, two, three, and . . . four . . . We _break_ our three eggs and _ _ _ _ _ _ them into the _ _ _ _ _ _. And, of course, _ _ _ _ _ _ are _ _ _ _ _ _ for you . . . and they're fun to eat . . . and not only that, but they're really _easy_. And . . . once we have our _ _ _ _ _ _ in the _ _ _ _ _ _, we . . . _ _ _ _ _ _ a little _ _ _ _ _ _. Where's the _ _ _ _ _ _, Janet?
Janet: In the _ _ _ _ _ _ – _ _ _ _ _ _ you!

Discuss your answers with a partner.

24

Activity 6

Complete the conversation with words from the list.

tomato	little
oil	add
put	frying pan
onion	left
right	salt
medium	ingredients

Dennis: Once we've got that done, we're ready to _ _ _ _ _ _ our other
_ _ _ _ _ _ . You'll need an _ _ _ _ _ _ , a green pepper, a _ _ _ _ _ _ , and
some _ _ _ _ _ _ and pepper, and some _ _ _ _ _ _ for the _ _ _ _ _ _ . The
frying pan, Janet?
Janet: The _ _ _ _ _ _ drawer.
Janet: Not the _ _ _ _ _ _ – the right!
Dennis: Our pan. OK, now what we do is, we add a little oil to the pan . . .
just a _ _ _ _ _ _ at the bottom here. There we go. And we _ _ _ _ _ _ that
on _ _ _ _ _ _ heat.

Discuss your answers with a partner.

Now watch the video and check your answers. (19:11 – 20:00)

Activity 7

Complete the conversation with words from the list.

that's it	month	first
hospital	over	what
better	hardest	three

Dennis: Don't forget to write for today's recipe.
Janet: _ _ _ _ _ _ , folks!
Dennis: Thank goodness, that's _ _ _ _ _ _ !
Janet: It's OK, Dennis. The _ _ _ _ _ _ time is always the _ _ _ _ _ _ . You'll
get _ _ _ _ _ _ .
Dennis: _ _ _ _ _ _ do you mean, "I'll get better"?
Janet: Arlene called again. She's going to be in the _ _ _ _ _ _ for a
_ _ _ _ _ _ . Looks like you'll be doing _ _ _ _ _ _ more shows, Dennis.
Dennis: Oh, no!

Discuss your answers with a partner.

Now watch the video and check your answers. (22:37 – 23:02)

Activity 1

ORDER THE EVENTS

Number these sentences in the correct order from 1 to 7.

☐ Arlene talks to Janet on the phone.
☐ Janet says: "Arlene's going to be in the hospital for a month."
☐ Dennis talks to Arlene on the phone.
☐ Janet tells Dennis: "You'll be doing three more shows."
☐ Dennis talks to his boss on the phone.
☐ Dennis tells Janet: "Thank goodness that's over!"
☐ Dennis says: "I'm not going to do that show."

Discuss your answers with a partner.

Activity 2

WHICH STEP COMES NEXT?

Write out the recipe for Dennis' omelet.

Method

_____

_____

_____

_____

_____

_____

_____

_____

_____

_____

_____

Chop the onion and put it in the pan.

Pour the egg and milk into the pan.

Break three eggs into a bowl.

Add the salt and pepper.

Simmer for three minutes.

Add the milk to the eggs.

Chop the green pepper and tomatoes.

Add a little parsley and tomato for color.

Add the green pepper and tomato to the onions.

Pour the oil into the pan and put it on medium heat.

Put the omelet on a plate.

Discuss your recipe with a partner.

Activity 3

ROLE PLAY

Read through the script silently. Then read out the script in pairs. The script is on page 59. Now role-play the story.

LANGUAGE CHECK

Complete the blanks with the correct form of the verb.

Dennis Johnson is a TV producer. For him today is a special day. Usually he
_ _ _ _ _ _ (direct) the cooking show. But today he is not directing the show.
He's going to cook on TV. Usually Dennis _ _ _ _ _ _ (get up) at 7:30. But
today is special. It's 6:30 a.m. and Dennis _ _ _ _ _ _ (get up). In the morning
Dennis's wife, Sue, always _ _ _ _ _ _ (cook) breakfast. But today Sue
_ _ _ _ _ _ (be) in Atlanta visiting her sister, so right now Dennis _ _ _ _ _ _
(make) breakfast for himself. Dennis _ _ _ _ _ _ (cook) hard-boiled eggs.
They _ _ _ _ _ _ (be) easy to do. It's 8:00 a.m.. Sometimes Dennis _ _ _ _ _ _
(walk) to work but today he _ _ _ _ _ _ (drive) because he _ _ _ _ _ _ (be) in a
hurry. It's 11:00 a.m.. Dennis and Janet _ _ _ _ _ _ (talk) about today's show.
It's 12:00. Dennis _ _ _ _ _ _ (cook) tacos on TV. He _ _ _ _ _ _ (chop) the
onions. Janet _ _ _ _ _ _ (tell) him to hurry. It's 6:00 p.m.. Dennis and Janet
_ _ _ _ _ _ (go) home. Dennis _ _ _ _ _ _ (give) Janet a ride home. Usually
Dennis _ _ _ _ _ _ (jog) after work but tonight he is too tired. It's 9:30.
Dennis _ _ _ _ _ _ (read) a cookbook in bed. He _ _ _ _ _ _ (think) about next
week's show.

Discuss your answers with a partner.

Learn these words before doing the READING RETELL.

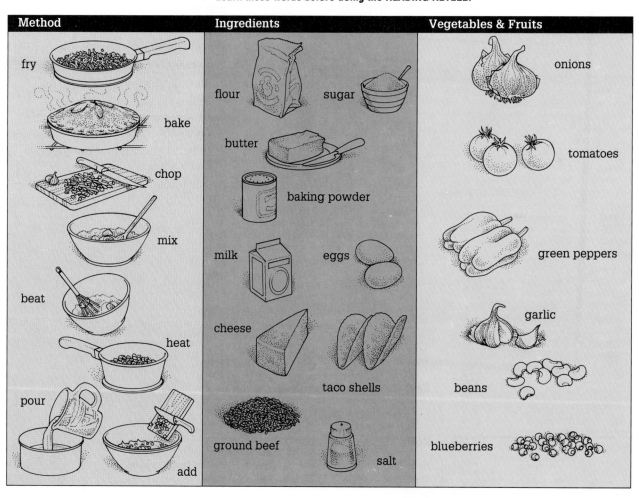

READING RETELL

STUDENT A

Read through the recipe and circle the ingredients and methods on page 26 needed to make tacos.

TACOS

Ingredients
1 pound (1/2 kilo) of
   ground beef
1 onion
2 green peppers
2 cups (1/2 liter) cooked beans
2 tomatoes
1/3 cup (75 ml) of oil
2 cups (1/2 liter) of grated
   cheese
Garlic
Salt
Taco shells

Method
1. Chop onions and garlic.
2. Fry onions, garlic and meat in oil and salt.
3. Heat beans in a small pan.
4. Put some of the meat mixture and beans onto each taco shell.
5. Now chop tomatoes, onions and green peppers into small pieces.
6. Put some tomatoes, onions, green peppers into the taco shells.
7. Cover with cheese.

⬛⬤ *Work in pairs. Student A reads out the ingredients and how to make Tacos to Student B, who makes notes on the outline provided. Student B then uses these notes to retell the recipe.*

Write your partner's recipe below.

BLUEBERRY CAKE

Ingredients

Method
1 Mix _ _ _ _ _ _ and sugar together in a _ _ _ _ _ _ .
2 Add _ _ _ _ _ _ the mixture and _ _ _ _ _ _ well.
3 Mix _ _ _ _ _ _ and baking powder together and _ _ _ _ _ _ them to the mixture.
4 Pour _ _ _ _ _ _ slowly into the mixture.
5 Add _ _ _ _ _ _ .
6 Pour _ _ _ _ _ _ mixture into a medium baking _ _ _ _ _ _ .
7 Bake at _ _ _ _ _ _ degrees for _ _ _ _ _ _ minutes.

STUDENT B

Read through the recipe and circle the ingredients and methods on page 26 needed to make Blueberry cake.

BLUEBERRY CAKE

Ingredients
1/4 cup (50 ml) soft butter
1/2 cup (125 ml) of sugar
1 egg
1 1/2 cups of flour
2 teaspoons (10 ml) baking
  powder
1/2 cup (125 ml) milk
1 cup (250 ml) of blueberries

Method
1. Mix butter and sugar together in a bowl.
2. Add egg to the mixture and beat well.
3. Mix flour and baking powder together and add them to the mixture.
4. Pour milk slowly into the mixture.
5. Add blueberries.
6. Pour cake mixture into a medium baking pan.
7. Bake at 375 degrees for 30 minutes.

Work in pairs. Student B reads out the ingredients and how to make Blueberry cake to Student A, who makes notes on the outline provided. Student A then uses these notes to retell the recipe.

Write your partner's recipe below.

TACOS

Ingredients

Method
1 Chop _ _ _ _ _ _ and garlic.
2 Fry _ _ _ _ _ _ , garlic and _ _ _ _ _ _ in oil and salt.
3 Heat beans in a small _ _ _ _ _ _ .
4 Put some of the _ _ _ _ _ _ mixture and _ _ _ _ _ _ onto each taco shell.
5 Now, _ _ _ _ _ _ tomatoes, _ _ _ _ _ _ and green peppers into small pieces.
6 Put some _ _ _ _ _ _ , _ _ _ _ _ _ and green peppers into the taco shells.
7 Cover with _ _ _ _ _ _ .

Functions

Now you can:

Introduce yourself	Hello, my name is Dennis Johnson.
Describe processes/ Give instructions	We take our 3 eggs and break them into a bowl. Next, we chop our onion. We add a little milk. Always remember to keep the beater on low.
Ask for information	What are we cooking? Where's the milk?
Express ability/inability	I can cook, but... I can't cook on TV.
Express likes	I love omelets. I love to cook.
Express sympathy	I'm sorry to hear that. All the best.

Structures

Present progressive	We're cooking Spanish omelets.
Negative:	I'm not doing that show.
Interrogative:	What are we cooking?
Future with 'will'	I'll tell him after the show. You'll need an onion. You'll get better.
Future with 'going to'	She's going to be in the hospital for a month. Who's going to do the show?
Imperative	Never hurry. Watch your pan. Get ready to add our other ingredients. Wait!
'can'/'can't'	I can cook, but... I can't do this . Arlene can't do the show.
Question words	Where are you? Where's the milk? What do you mean? What are we cooking? Who's going to do the show?
Prepositions of location	*On* the counter *behind* you. *In* the fridge. *At* the bottom.

Words and expressions

recipe	pie	low (heat)	to flip
ingredients	pizza	medium	to cry
mixture		white	to watch
omelet	counter	round	to forget
eggs	fridge		to make mistakes
milk	(refrigerator)		to write
onion	drawer	to cook	
tomato	frying pan	to chop	
green pepper	electric beater	to add	What a great idea!
salt	hand beater	to break	There we go.
pepper	plate	to burn	Here we go.
oil	bowl	to hurry	That's no good.
parsley		to heat	I'm not ready.
		to simmer	Thank goodness!

4 Vacation for two?

Look at these ads for vacation packages. Then answer the questions.

How much does the ski vacation cost?

What is the name of the ski resort?

How many nights does the package include?

Does the package include all meals?

Does it cost extra to have ski lessons?

What should you do if you want more information?

How much is the package to Acapulco?

Where does the plane leave from?

Does the package include hotel accommodation?

Does the package include meals?

On what days of the week can you leave?

What is the name of the travel agency?

What about you?

Which vacation do you prefer? Why?

BOULDER Colorado USA

The Alpine Ski Resort

$495

PACKAGE INCLUDES

▷ hotel accommodation for 7 days/6 nights
▷ 7 days skiing
▷ 2 meals per day

NOT INCLUDED

▷ ski lessons
▷ equipment rental (skis, boots, poles)

For more information, call Steve at 'Super Travel' 731-4692.

If you love to ski, come to the Rockies.

Acapulco MEXICO

SUN, SEA AND SAND

at Club Paradise

2 weeks for only **$1,019***

PACKAGE INCLUDES

● round trip airfare from Toronto to Acapulco
● hotel accommodation for 14 nights
● transportation between airport and hotel
● free watersports (swimming, sailing, water-skiing)

For more information, call Sally at 'Fast Travel' 631-9024.

* departures on Tuesdays & Sundays

While you watch	VIDEO 4 ▪ Vacation for two?

Activity 1

Here are the main characters in the video.

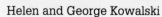
Helen and George Kowalski   Travel Agent

Read the questions. Then watch the video and try to get the answers.

What does Helen want to do on her vacation?

What does George want to do on his vacation?

Does the travel agent help them?

 Watch the video. (23:30 – 28:43)

Activity 2

 Read through these statements and in groups decide if they are true or false. Put a check mark in the box. If the answer is 'False', give the correct information.

		True	False
1	George and Helen want to go on vacation.	☐	☐
2	George loves to ski.	☐	☐
3	Helen loves hot sun and sandy beaches.	☐	☐
4	George thinks he's getting fat.	☐	☐
5	Helen thinks beaches are boring.	☐	☐
6	George wants to see snow during his vacation.	☐	☐
7	The travel agent suggests separate vacations.	☐	☐
8	George chooses a place in Mexico.	☐	☐
9	Helen chooses a place in Colorado.	☐	☐
10	George needs to rent a car.	☐	☐
11	The ski resort is right on the mountain.	☐	☐
12	George and Helen don't really want to take separate vacations.	☐	☐
13	In the end, George and Helen decide to go to Hawaii.	☐	☐
14	In Hawaii the hotel is located right on the mountain.	☐	☐
15	The hotel has scuba diving.	☐	☐
16	The travel agent gives George and Helen their tickets right away.	☐	☐
17	The travel agent thinks she should get a job as a full-time marriage counsellor.	☐	☐

 Now, watch the video and check your answers. (23:30 – 28:43)

After you watch, discuss your answers in your group.

While you watch	VIDEO 4 ▪ Vacation for two?

Activity 3 📺

Watch the video and answer your teacher's questions. (23:00 – 23:44)

Activity 4 📺

Watch this part of the video twice and fill in the missing words. (23:45 – 24:08)

Helen: Fine. I'll go alone.
George: Helen!
Helen: I'm _ _ _ _ _ _, George. If you _ _ _ _ _ _ to come, I will go by myself.
George: Don't be silly.
Helen: I'm not being _ _ _ _ _ _!
George: Helen, please you're _ _ _ _ _ _.
Helen: I'm _ _ _ _ _ _.
Agent: Excuse me!
Helen & George: What?
Agent: Can I _ _ _ _ _ _?
George: I doubt it.
Helen: We want to book our _ _ _ _ _ _.
George: _ _ _ _ _ _ vacation, you mean.
Helen: George! Why are you being so _ _ _ _ _ _?
Agent: Please, _ _ _ _ _ _. I'm sure I can help.

📀 *Discuss your answers with a partner.*

Activity 5 📺

Watch the video and answer your teacher's questions. (25:12 – 25:36)

Activity 6

Complete the conversation with the words from the list.

rent	decision
places	brochure
airport	guess
beach	to book
expensive	openings
ski resort	dates
transportation	

Agent: So, have you made your _ _ _ _ _ _?
George: A lot of these places are too _ _ _ _ _ _, but this one in Mexico
  looks good.
Helen: I like the _ _ _ _ _ _ in Colorado.
Agent: OK. Can I get your _ _ _ _ _ _, please?
Helen: Sure, February 10th to the 24th. Forget Valentine's Day.
Agent: You're in luck. I have _ _ _ _ _ _ on those dates for both _ _ _ _ _ _.
  Do you want _ _ _ _ _ _ them?
George: Yeah, I _ _ _ _ _ _ so.
Agent: OK. Now, will you be needing to _ _ _ _ _ _ a car while you're there?
George: Well, it says here in the _ _ _ _ _ _ that the hotel provides free
  _ _ _ _ _ _ from the _ _ _ _ _ _, and it's right on the _ _ _ _ _ _.

📀 *Compare your answers with a partner.*

📺 *Now watch the video and check your answers.* (25:37 – 26:10)

While you watch	VIDEO 4 ▪ Vacation for two?

Activity 7

Complete the conversation with the words from the list.

suggestion	perfect
expensive	tickets
terrific	package
skiing	hotel
vacations	sailing
too	great
take	

Agent: Listen, you two, I don't think you really want to go on separate vacations, do you? I've got another _ _ _ _ _ _ . I just called the Hawaiian travel bureau and I can get a _ _ _ _ _ _ to the island that includes four days of _ _ _ _ _ _ on Mount Mauna Kea. What do you think?

Helen: Oh, it sounds _ _ _ _ _ _ !

George: Yeah, but is it _ _ _ _ _ _ ?

Agent: No more expensive than paying for separate _ _ _ _ _ _ .

Helen: Is the _ _ _ _ _ _ on the beach?

Agent: It sure is. There's swimming and water skiing and _ _ _ _ _ _ .

George: Scuba diving?

Agent: Sure. They have scuba diving lessons, _ _ _ _ _ _ .

Helen: Oh, it sounds _ _ _ _ _ _ . We'll _ _ _ _ _ _ it.

Agent: _ _ _ _ _ _ ! Listen, your _ _ _ _ _ _ will be ready in about a week's time.

Discuss your answers with a partner.

Now watch the video and check your answers. (27:38 – 28:13)

Activity 1

WHO SAID THIS?

Write H for Helen, G for George and A for agent.

☐ We went skiing last year.

☐ You need the exercise.

☐ Please, have a seat. I'm sure I can help.

☐ I want the hot sun and sandy beaches.

☐ Beaches are so boring.

☐ Sure, a lot of married couples do it.

☐ Can I get your full name, please?

☐ I don't mind skiing really.

☐ I'm not getting mad.

☐ Yeah, but is it expensive?

Discuss your answers with a partner.

Activity 2

WHICH LINE COMES NEXT?

Match the sentences in Column A with the replies in Column B.

COLUMN A	COLUMN B
Don't be silly.	Sure. February 10th to the 24th.
Can I help you?	George and Helen Kowalski.
Now, where is it you'd like to go?	I'm not being silly!
Beaches are so boring.	No more expensive than paying for separate vacations.
Can I get your dates, please?	So is skiing.
Can I get your full name please?	I doubt it.
Is it expensive?	My pleasure.
Thanks very much.	Florida.

Discuss your answers with a partner.

Activity 3

ROLE PLAY

Read through the script silently. Then get into groups of three and read out the script. The script is on page 60. Now role-play the story.

Follow up | VIDEO 4 ▪ Vacation for two?

LANGUAGE CHECK

Activity 1

Complete the conversation.

Travel Agent: Good morning. Can _ _ _ _ _ _ ?
Customer: Yes, I'd like to book a vacation.
Travel Agent: Where would you _ _ _ _ _ _ ?
Customer: Mexico or Florida.
Travel Agent: Well, I have a one-week package to Florida.
Customer: _ _ _ _ _ _ cost?
Travel Agent: $499.
Customer: _ _ _ _ _ _ include?
Travel Agent: It includes airfare and hotel accommodation for one week.
Customer: It sounds _ _ _ _ _ _ . I'll take it.
Travel Agent: _ _ _ _ _ _ to rent a car?
Customer: No, I don't like to drive when I'm on vacation. _ _ _ _ _ _ the tickets be ready?
Travel Agent: In a week's time.

Discuss your answers with a partner.

Activity 2

Complete the blanks using the Simple Past tense.

George and Helen Kowalski returned from their vacation two days ago. George is calling the travel agency to complain about their vacation.

Travel Agent: Good afternoon, Lost Horizons Travel.
George: This is George Kowalski. I _ _ _ _ _ _ (book) a vacation with your company a few weeks ago.
Travel Agent: Oh yes, Mr. Kowalski. How _ _ _ _ _ _ (be) your vacation?
George: Terrible!
Travel Agent: Well, where _ _ _ _ _ _ you _ _ _ _ _ _ (go)?
George: Hawaii.
Travel Agent: How _ _ _ _ _ _ (be) the weather?
George: Awful! It _ _ _ _ _ _ (rain) almost every day.
Travel Agent: Maybe you _ _ _ _ _ _ (be) just unlucky.
George: No, I don't think so. Look, the weather _ _ _ _ _ _ (not be) the only problem. When we _ _ _ _ _ _ (arrive) in Hawaii, there _ _ _ _ _ _ (be) no transportation from the airport to the hotel. We _ _ _ _ _ _ (have to) take a taxi. It _ _ _ _ _ _ (cost) $25. When we _ _ _ _ _ _ (get) to the hotel, we _ _ _ _ _ _ (have) another surprise. The hotel _ _ _ _ _ _ (not be) on the beach. In fact, it _ _ _ _ _ _ (take) us 20 minutes to walk there. So, I _ _ _ _ _ _ (rent) a car. Then, when we _ _ _ _ _ _ (go) to the beach, we _ _ _ _ _ _ (find) that the hotel _ _ _ _ _ _ (not have) any watersports. But, the worst surprise _ _ _ _ _ _ (come) in the second week. Our four days of skiing were cancelled. And now, I want my money back. Let me speak to the manager.
Travel Agent: I'm sorry, he's not here.
George: Where is he?
Travel Agent: He's on vacation in Hawaii!

Discuss your answers with a partner.

READING RETELL

Read Text A and answer the questions.

1 Does George like his vacation?

2 What did the brochure say about the weather?

3 What is the weather like today?

4 What did George and Helen do yesterday?

5 How long did they wait at the airport?

6 What did they have to do?

7 How much did the ride to the hotel cost?

8 Is the hotel on Waikiki Beach?

9 What did they have to do?

10 Does George like the food?

11 What does Helen want to bring home?

12 What was the problem the first day?

13 What is George going to do when he gets home?

14 Why can't they go skiing?

15 Does George like skiing?

🔲🔲 **Check your answers with a partner.**

Retell your letter to a student with Text B.

TEXT A   **Letter from Hawaii**

Club Paradise
Honolulu
February 14th

Dear Mom,

We are having a terrible vacation. Everything is going wrong. The brochure said the weather is always hot and sunny in Hawaii. Well, today it's raining. It rained yesterday, the day before and the day before that. Yesterday we went shopping in Honolulu and guess what? We had to buy an umbrella.

Our problems started at the airport in Hawaii. The brochure said free transportation from the airport to the hotel. Helen and I waited for two hours, but nobody came. So, we had to take a taxi. The ride to the hotel cost $25!

The hotel is another problem. The brochure said the hotel was on Waikiki Beach. This isn't true. The hotel is a twenty-minute walk from the beach. So, we had to rent a car. It's very expensive - $350 a week!

The food is a real problem too. They give you fruit for breakfast—seven different kinds! Helen loves it. She wants to bring home a box of pineapples!

The first day of our vacation, I wanted to go scuba diving. After breakfast, we went to the beach. But, guess what? There were no watersports.... No sailing, no waterskiing, no scuba diving... nothing! When we get home, I'm going to kill the travel agent! Helen says "Hello".

Love, George

P.S. Remember our package included skiing? Well, there isn't enough snow on the mountain. So, our four days of skiing are cancelled. Helen is disappointed, but I'm happy. I hate skiing.

Read Text B and answer the questions.

1 Why does Helen like Hawaii?

2 Where did they spend the first few days?

3 What does Helen tell us about Honolulu?

4 What time did Helen get up the first morning?

5 What did she do?

6 What did George do?

7 What did Helen eat for breakfast yesterday?

8 What did George have for breakfast?

9 How did Helen and George get to the Big Island?

10 Why was George angry?

11 What did they visit yesterday?

12 What did George take as a souvenir?

13 What kind of beaches can you find on the Big Island?

14 What did George want to do at Black Sand Beach?

15 What did the brochure say?

▣▣ **Check your answers with a partner.**

Retell your letter to a student with Text A.

TEXT B   **Another letter from Hawaii**

Big Island Hotel
February 19th

Dear Karen,

Here we are in Hawaii, I love it! Everything is so green and there are flowers everywhere.

When we arrived, we spent the first few days in Honolulu. Honolulu is a big city – more than 350,000 people. We had a nice hotel near Waikiki Beach. Waikiki is the most popular beach for tourists. The first morning I got up early – 6 a.m. – and went for a walk on the beach. Of course, George didn't get up. He slept until 10! The walk on the beach was great.

One of the best things here is the fresh fruit - pineapples, bananas, oranges, grapefruit…. Yesterday for breakfast I ate a whole pineapple! It was delicious. George doesn't like pineapple. He had his usual breakfast - two fried eggs, toast and coffee!

I didn't know it, but Hawaii is not just one island. It's really a group of islands. Right now we're on the Big Island. To get here, we had to take a plane from Honolulu. George was angry because we had to pay more money. Yesterday we visited the volcanoes in the national park. We rented a car and drove around the park. It took all day. George loved the volcanoes. He took some pieces of volcanic rock as a souvenir.

Guess what? On the Big Island there are beaches with black sand. Yes, it's true! The black sand comes from the volcanic rock. We stopped at Black Sand Beach to take photos. It was so beautiful! There were palm trees all along the beach. George wanted to go swimming but the brochure said there were sharks in the water… Of course, George got mad as usual. He complains about everything!

Bye for now. See you when we get back.

Your friend,
Helen

P.S. We took lots of photos of everything! We'll show them to you when we get home.

Functions

Now you can:

Offer help	Can I help you? I'm sure I can help.
Express desires	We want to book our winter vacation. I want to go skiing.
Request information	Can I get your dates, please? Do you want to book them? Can I get your full names, please? Is it expensive? Is the hotel on the beach? How about you?
Express opinions	It sounds perfect! It sounds great! Beaches are so boring. I like the ski resort in Colorado. The one in Mexico looks good.
Make suggestions	Have you thought of taking separate vacations? I've got another suggestion.

Structures

Present progressive	You're shouting.
Negative:	I'm not getting fat. I'm not shouting. I'm not being silly. I'm not getting mad.
Interrogative:	Why are you being so difficult?
Simple past	We went skiing last year. I was wrong. It rained yesterday.
Future with 'will'	I'll go alone. I'll have your ticket in a week's time. I'll call you right back. We'll take it.
'want'/'want to do'	I want the hot sun. I don't want to go to Acapulco by myself. Do you want to book them?
'should'	We should do what you want to do. Maybe we should finish those separate bookings.
Information questions	Where is it you'd like to go? What's wrong with that?

Words and expressions

vacation	travel bureau	sailing	to provide	Come on!	Sure.
brochure	place	swimming	to suntan	Fine.	OK.
package	resort	scuba diving	to bake	I'm serious.	That's perfect.
price	hotel	beach		Don't be silly!	Have a
dates	airport	mountain	free	Excuse me.	wonderful
flight	transportation		expensive	Great!	vacation!
tickets	sun	to pay	hot	Let's see . . .	My pleasure.
details	snow	to include	perfect	That's right.	'Bye now . . .
booking	skiing	to leave		Look!	
opening	water skiing	to return		Listen!	

Maxie's revenge

Look at these pictures.

BANK ROBBER

PICKPOCKET

SHOPLIFTER

COUNTERFEITER

Now complete the sentence with the correct phrase from the box.

1 A bank robber is a person who _ _ _ _ _ _ _ _ _ _ _ _ _ _ _ _ _ .
2 A pickpocket is a person who _ _ _ _ _ _ _ _ _ _ _ _ _ _ _ _ _ .
3 A shoplifter is a person who _ _ _ _ _ _ _ _ _ _ _ _ _ _ _ _ _ .
4 A counterfeiter is a person who _ _ _ _ _ _ _ _ _ _ _ _ _ _ _ _ .

makes false money
steals from a store
steals from someone's pocket or purse
steals money from a bank

Alvin "Butch" Blackman
- 26 years old
- 1 meter 87 (6 feet 3 inches)
- 64 kilos (140 pounds)
- curly black hair, brown eyes
- mustache
- scar on left cheek
- WANTED for bank robbery

Samuel "Poison" Peterson
- 35 years old
- 1 meter 75 (5 feet 10 inches)
- 82 kilos (180 pounds)
- straight brown hair, brown eyes
- eye patch left eye
- WANTED for shoplifting

Winston "Crusher" Curry
- 41 years old
- 1 meter 60 (5 feet 4 inches)
- 100 kilos (220 pounds)
- bald, blue eyes
- tattoo, right arm
- WANTED for pickpocketing

Herman "Brains" Barrie
- 21 years old
- 1 meter 65 (5 feet 6 inches)
- 64 kilos (140 pounds)
- blond hair, blue eyes
- glasses
- WANTED for counterfeiting

These men are criminals. They are 'Wanted' by the police.

Look at the pictures and read the description of each criminal. Then write the name of the criminal under his picture.

Discuss your answers with a partner.

Now answer these questions about the 'wanted' men. Put a check mark by the correct answer.

1 Crusher ☐ is / ☒ isn't taller than Brains.

2 Poison ☐ weighs / ☐ doesn't weigh more than Butch.

3 Crusher ☐ is / ☐ isn't the oldest.

4 Butch ☐ is / ☐ isn't wanted for counterfeiting.

5 Poison ☐ wears / ☒ doesn't wear glasses.

6 Brains ☐ has / ☐ doesn't have a mustache.

7 Crusher ☐ has / ☐ doesn't have a tattoo on his left arm.

8 Brains ☐ has / ☐ doesn't have blond hair.

9 Poison ☐ is / ☐ isn't bald.

Discuss your answers with a partner.

Activity 1

Here are the main characters in the video.

Maxie Gardiner   Bob Desmond   Al Malloy   Mrs. Colombo

Read the questions. Then watch the video and try to get the answers.

Who is Maxie?

Who are Desmond and Malloy?

Does Maxie go to jail?

What is "Maxie's Revenge"?

 Watch the video. (29:06 – 36:09)

Activity 2

Read through these statements and in groups decide if they are true or false.
Put a check mark in the box. If the answer is 'False', write the correct information.

		True	False
1	The detective tells Maxie to empty his pockets.	☒	☐
2	Maxie has four wallets.	☐	☒
3	The wallets are all Maxie's.	☐	☒
4	Maxie is a taxi driver, a lawyer and a mechanic.	☐	☒
5	The police are going to get Maxie's fingerprints.	☒	☐
6	Maxie is really forty years old.	☐	☒
7	Maxie is a pickpocket.	☒	☐
8	Maxie was in jail for two years.	☐	☐
9	Mrs. Colombo could not identify Maxie.	☐	☒
10	Mrs. Colombo had a mouse in her purse.	☐	☒
11	Desmond and Malloy go to Joe's Steak House for lunch.	☒	☐
12	Desmond and Malloy had steak for supper.	☐	☐
13	The bill was $52.	☐	☐
14	Malloy could not find his wallet.	☐	☐
15	Desmond found his wallet.	☒	☒
16	The note said, "I hope you boys like washing dishes."	☐	☐

 Now, watch the video again and check your answers. (29:06 – 36:09)

After you watch, discuss your answers in your group.

Activity 3

Watch this part of the video twice and fill in the missing information. (30:21 – 31:15)

Name	Age	Hair	Eyes	Height	Weight	Occupation	Marital Status
William Lukeman	49			1 meter 55			married
George Taylor		brown				lawyer	
Ken Cooper	22				80 kilos		

Discuss your answers with a partner.

Activity 4

Watch the video and answer your teacher's questions. (32:27 – 33:23)

Activity 5

Watch this part of the video twice and fill in the missing words. (32:42 – 33:52)

Desmond: So, your name really is Maxie Gardiner. Maxwell Gardiner,
_ _ _ _ _ _, 1 meter 65, 75 kilos, _ _ _ _ _ _and divorced twice, no fixed
address. First arrest was in 1962. Total of five arrests in all. _ _ _ _ _ _ in
jail. Congratulations, Maxie, you're well-known. You're the _ _ _ _ _ _
pickpocket in the country.
Maxie: That's right, _ _ _ _ _ _ . I'm _ _ _ _ _ _ .
Desmond: Well, you made _ _ _ _ _ _ . You came to Montreal and met us.
Bring in Mrs. Colombo.
Malloy: Mrs. Colombo.
Desmond: _ _ _ _ _ _ , Mrs. Colombo? Take your time. Look carefully.
Mrs. Colombo: I don't have to _ _ _ _ _ _ , young man. That's him. I'm
_ _ _ _ _ _ . That's the thief.
Desmond: Are you absolutely sure?
Mrs. Colombo: Yes, I am. I'm absolutely sure. That's the man.
Desmond: _ _ _ _ _ _ , Mrs. Colombo. Take him away.

Discuss your answers with a partner.

Activity 6

Complete the conversation with the words from the list.

vacation	dinner	too bad	jail
smart	purse	lucky	finished

Malloy: Well, Maxie, you're _ _ _ _ _ _ . We were just too _ _ _ _ _ _ for you.
Maxie: Smart, hah! You were just _ _ _ _ _ _ ! Crazy old woman! A
  mousetrap in her _ _ _ _ _ _ !
Malloy: Well, _ _ _ _ _ _ for you, Maxie boy. You're going to _ _ _ _ _ _ for a
  nice, long _ _ _ _ _ _ . And we're going to Joe's Steak House for _ _ _ _ _ _ .

Discuss your answers with a partner.

Now watch the video and check your answers. (34:30 – 34:54)

Activity 7

Complete the conversation with the words from the list.

bill	great	pay	how much
find	station	supper	water

Desmond: _ _ _ _ _ _ steak, Malloy. That was good work today.
Malloy: Yeah.
Desmond: I wonder what our friend Maxie's having for _ _ _ _ _ _ tonight.
Malloy: Bread and _ _ _ _ _ _ , I hope. Waitress! Waitress! The _ _ _ _ _ _ ,
  please.
Desmond: It's a good restaurant here.
Malloy: Yeah.
(*The waitress brings the bill.*)
Malloy: Thank you.
Desmond: _ _ _ _ _ _ is it?
Malloy: Forty-two dollars.
Desmond: OK, we'll _ _ _ _ _ _ it and leave.
Malloy: My wallet! I can't _ _ _ _ _ _ my wallet! I probably left it at the
  _ _ _ _ _ _ . Can you pay?

Discuss your answers with a partner.

Now watch the video and check your answers. (34:55 – 35:36)

Activity 8

Watch the video and answer your teacher's questions. (35:37 – 36:09)

44

After you watch   VIDEO 5 ▪ Maxie's revenge

Activity 1

WHO SAID THIS?

Write D for Desmond, M for Maxie and C for Mrs. Colombo.

☐ OK, empty your pockets and sit down.
☐ Why not? It's a nice name.
☐ OK, Malloy, take him to the cell.
☐ That's right, cop. I'm the best.
☐ That's him. I'm sure it's him.
☐ Why did you have a mousetrap in your purse?
☐ A man stole my wallet.
☐ You were just lucky.
☐ Great steak, Malloy.
☐ Hey, what's this?

Discuss your answers with a partner.

Activity 2

WHICH LINE COMES NEXT?

Match the sentences in Column A with the replies in Column B.

COLUMN A

Your name is William Lukeman,
your name is George Taylor,
and your name is also Ken Cooper.

My name is Maxie Gardiner.

Is this the man, Mrs. Colombo?
Look carefully. Take your time.

Why did you have a mousetrap in
your purse?

Well, Maxie, you're finished. We
were too smart for you.

How much is it?

Can you pay?

What does the note say?

COLUMN B

Smart, hah! You were just lucky!

It says, "I hope you boys like
washing dishes".

I was robbed last year, officer.

Forty-two dollars.

Well, I like variety in my life.

I don't have to take my time, young
man. That's him.

We'll check that name out.

No problem.

Discuss your answers with a partner.

Activity 3

ROLE PLAY

*Read through the script silently. Then get into groups of four and read out the script.
The script is on page 61. Now role-play the story.*

Follow up   VIDEO 5 ▪ Maxie's revenge

LANGUAGE CHECK

Activity 1

Fill in the blanks with the Simple Past tense form of the verb.

The owner of Joe's Steak House called the police because Desmond and Malloy couldn't pay their bill. Desmond and Malloy are talking to the police chief.

Chief: What's going on, you two?
Desmond: It's a long story, Chief. You see, yesterday we _ _ _ _ _ _ (catch) an important criminal.
Chief: Who _ _ _ _ _ _ you _ _ _ _ _ _ (catch)?
Desmond: Maxie Gardiner, the number one pickpocket in the country.
Malloy: Yeah, he _ _ _ _ _ _ (make) one big mistake. He _ _ _ _ _ _ (come) here and he _ _ _ _ _ (meet) us.
Chief: What _ _ _ _ _ _ Maxie _ _ _ _ _ _ (do)?
Desmond: He _ _ _ _ _ _ (rob) an old woman. But, she _ _ _ _ _ _ (have) a mousetrap in her purse.
Chief: A mousetrap! Why _ _ _ _ _ _ she _ _ _ _ _ _ (have) a mousetrap in her purse?
Malloy: Because last year someone _ _ _ _ _ _ (steal) her wallet.
Desmond: Anyway, we _ _ _ _ _ _ (go) to Joe's Steak House. We _ _ _ _ _ _ (eat) steak and ...
Chief: OK, OK. But why _ _ _ _ _ _ you _ _ _ _ _ _ (not, pay) your bill?
Desmond: Well, uh... we _ _ _ _ _ _ (not, can) find our wallets and then I _ _ _ _ _ _ (find) a note in my pocket.
Chief: What _ _ _ _ _ _ the note _ _ _ _ _ _ (say)?
Desmond: Here it is, Chief.
(*The chief reads Maxie's note.*)
Chief: So, that's why you _ _ _ _ _ _ (not, have) any money! Well it looks like Maxie _ _ _ _ _ _ (get) his revenge.
Malloy: Yeah, that sneaky little creep!

◐● *Discuss your answers with a partner.*

Activity 2

Fill in the blanks with the correct form of the verb. Use the Simple Past or the Past Progressive.

Maxie's capture

Maxie is a pickpocket. One day he _ _ _ _ _ _ (stand) in a subway station. He _ _ _ _ _ _ (look) for someone to rob. Then he _ _ _ _ _ (see) an old lady. She _ _ _ _ _ _ (look) in her purse for her subway tickets. Maxie _ _ _ _ _ _ (walk) over and _ _ _ _ _ _ (stand) beside her. When she _ _ _ _ _ _ (not, look) he _ _ _ _ _ _ (put) his hand in her purse. Suddenly he _ _ _ _ _ _ (scream). She _ _ _ _ _ _ (have) a mousetrap in her purse! He _ _ _ _ _ _ (start) to run. He _ _ _ _ _ _ (run) to the exit when he _ _ _ _ _ _ (see) two policemen in front of him. Behind him, the old lady _ _ _ _ _ _ (scream) and people _ _ _ _ _ _ (shout), "Stop, thief!" Maxie stopped. When a policeman _ _ _ _ _ _ (arrest) him, Maxie _ _ _ _ _ _ (smile). "Why are you smiling?" _ _ _ _ _ _ (say) the policeman. "Because I'm thinking about the nice long vacation I'm going to have", _ _ _ _ _ _ (reply) Maxie.

◐● *Discuss your answers with a partner.*

READING RETELL

Read Text A and answer the questions.

1 When did the robbery take place? Where?

2 How many cars did the train have?

3 What was inside the second car?

4 Why did the engineer stop the train?

5 What did he do?

6 Was the telephone working?

7 What did he see near the third car?

8 What happened next?

9 How many men jumped on the train?

10 What did they do?

11 What did the robbers begin doing at the bridge?

12 What time did they leave?

13 How much money did they escape with?

14 Where did the story appear?

◖◉ *Check your answers with a partner.*

Retell your story to a student with Text B.

Text A   **The Great Train Robbery**

At 3:00 a.m. on August 8, 1963 a train was travelling through the countryside of England. The train had thirteen cars. Inside the second car there were 128 bags of money. The train was bringing the money to a bank in London.

At a few minutes past three, the engineer saw a red light ahead. He stopped the train and went to see what was wrong. He didn't see anything, so he went to the telephone near the track to ask if there was a problem. The telephone wasn't working. Something was wrong! Then he saw a man near the third car. But before he could do anything, two men knocked him down.

Eleven men jumped on the train. First, they disconnected the last ten cars. Then they ordered the engineer to drive to a bridge over a road. Trucks were waiting under the bridge. The robbers began throwing bags of money into the trucks. They worked quickly. They knew exactly when the next train was coming. At 3:45 the leader looked at his watch and said, "That's enough, boys. It's time to go." The robbers escaped with two and a half million pounds, or almost six million dollars.

The story appeared in newspapers and magazines all around the world. Soon it became one of the most famous robberies of all time. Today we call it 'The Great Train Robbery'.

Read Text B and answer the questions.

1 How old is Donna?

2 Who is her father?

3 How did Donna always go to school?

4 What happened one day?

5 Why did the kidnappers phone Donna's father?

6 Did the police find Donna immediately?

7 When and where did the woman find the wallet?

8 What did she do with it?

9 What did the police find in the wallet?

10 What did the police do?

11 How many people did the police arrest?

12 Where did they find Donna?

13 What was she doing?

14 Was she hurt?

15 What did her father do?

🔘 *Check your answers with a partner.*

Retell your story to a student with Text A.

TEXT B   **Crime Does Not Pay**

Donna Black is six years old. She is the daughter of a millionaire. On April 9 Donna went to school as usual. She always went by car. But that morning when the car arrived at the school, three men were waiting. When Donna opened the door of the car, the men grabbed her. They pushed her into another car and took her to an apartment. Then they telephoned her father. They asked him for ten million dollars. They said, "Pay the money or we'll kill the girl." The police immediately began looking for little Donna. They worked day and night, but they found nothing.

Then eight days later, a woman found a wallet in the street and took it to the police. In the wallet the police found a note. The note asked for money from Donna's father. The wallet belonged to one of the kidnappers! His address was inside! Quickly the police went to the apartment. They broke down the door and rushed in. They arrested three men and a woman. Then they found Donna in another room. She was watching TV. Donna was not hurt.

A policeman took Donna to her home. Her mother and father were waiting for her. Her father cried with happiness. Donna said, "I'm fine, Daddy. Don't cry." Her father said, "We suffered for eight days, but now our little girl is back."

Functions

Now you can:

Express personal information	Your name is William Lukeman, age 49, brown hair, brown eyes, 70 kilos. Your name is also Ken Cooper, age 22, blond hair, blue eyes.
Request information	Who are you? How much is it? Why did you have a mousetrap in your purse?
Give orders/instructions	Empty your pockets and sit down. Answer the question. Take him to a cell.
Agree	Sure. That's for sure. That's right.
Express praise	Great steak, Malloy. That was good work. Good restaurant here.
Express gratitude	Thank you. Thanks again.
Respond to gratitude	Not at all. It's my pleasure.

Structures

Simple past	You made a big mistake. You came to Montreal. A man stole my wallet. We were just too smart for you.
Interrogative:	Why did you have a mousetrap in your purse?
Future with 'will'	We'll get his fingerprints. We'll find out who he is. Maybe he'll remember who he is.
Negative:	It won't happen again.
Imperative	Take him away. Bring in Mrs. Colombo. Let's go. Look carefully.
Question words	Who are you? Why did you have a mousetrap in your purse? How much is it? What does the note say?

Words and expressions

police station	mistake	to steal	Come on.
detective (cop)	note	to rob	No problem!
thief	address	to go to jail	Let's see . . .
pockets	lawyer	to arrest	Tell me . . .
pickpocket	taxi-driver	to find (out)	Oh no!
criminal	car mechanic	to bring in	Congratulations.
finger	restaurant	to check out	That sneaky
fingerprints	dinner	to answer	little creep!
handcuffs	supper	to wash	
wallet	steak		
purse	bread	single	
jail	water	married	
cell	bill	divorced	
arrest	dishes		
year			

49

6 Getting in shape

Here are some activities people do to get in shape. Write the name of the activity in the blank space. Work in pairs.

basketball swimming football baseball
skating tennis golf aerobics
bowling hockey karate weight lifting
soccer skiing bicycling jogging

Ask these questions to three students. Write their answers in the chart. Look at the example.

	Example	Student A	Student B	Student C
Name				
1 Do you like exercise?	yes			
2 What kind of exercise do you do?	jogging			
3 Where do you exercise?	in the park			
4 How often do you exercise?	3 times a week			
5 How long do you exercise?	half an hour			
6 Do you exercise alone or with other people?	alone			
7 What kind of shape are you in? poor fair good excellent	good			

Activity 1

Here are the main characters in the video.

| Joe | Frankie | Rocky | Carla |

Read the questions. Then watch the video and try to get the answers.

Where are Joe and Frankie?

Where does Joe go?

What does Joe do there?

Who is Carla?

Watch the video. (36:39 – 43:53)

Activity 2

Read through these statements and in groups decide if they are true or false.
Put a check mark in the box. If the answer is 'False', give the correct information.

		True	False
1	Joe doesn't get any exercise.	☐	☐
2	Frankie goes to the gym every day.	☐	☐
3	Joe is eating cheesecake.	☐	☐
4	Rocky used to be a boxer.	☐	☐
5	Joe was trying to lift 45 kilos.	☐	☐
6	Rocky told Joe to start slowly.	☐	☐
7	Rocky owns the gym.	☐	☐
8	Joe is 27 years old.	☐	☐
9	Joe has to lose at least 15 kilos.	☐	☐
10	Joe's last regular exercise was six months ago.	☐	☐
11	Joe had a medical check-up last year.	☐	☐
12	Joe is in terrible shape.	☐	☐
13	Joe rode the bike for 25 minutes.	☐	☐
14	Rocky says Joe should exercise at least twice a week.	☐	☐
15	Rocky says Joe should exercise for 20 minutes to half an hour.	☐	☐
16	Joe did twenty sit-ups.	☐	☐
17	Joe met his old girlfriend at Rocky's gym.	☐	☐
18	Carla is Rocky's girlfriend now.	☐	☐

Now watch the video again and check your answers. (36:39 – 43:53)

After you watch, discuss your answers in your group.

Activity 3

Watch this part of the video twice and fill in the missing words. (36:50 – 38:00)

Frankie: The bill, please. Come on, Joe, take it easy with the cheesecake.
Joe: I'm telling you, Frankie, I _ _ _ _ _ _ .
Frankie: Well, you don't look so good either.
Joe: Thank you.
Frankie: Don't you get any _ _ _ _ _ _ ?
Joe: No, not since Carla left. I'm _ _ _ _ _ _ . I work all day.
Frankie: You eat, don't you?
Joe: Yeah, so?
Frankie: So if you've got the time to eat, you've _ _ _ _ _ _ .
Joe: Since when did you become Mr. Fitness?
Frankie: Hey, I started _ _ _ _ _ _ _ last year. I go every day now.
Joe: _ _ _ _ _ _ ?
Frankie: Uh-huh. Come on. Lunch is on me.
Joe: Frankie, Frankie, I'm not finished my cheesecake. Where do you _ _ _ _ _ _ ?
Frankie: Rocky's Gym. Some guy named Rocky De Nucci owns it.
Joe: Rocky De Nucci! What is this guy – _ _ _ _ _ _ ?
Frankie: Nah! I think he used to be some kind of tennis player.
Joe: Oh no, not another tennis player!
Frankie: Will you _ _ _ _ _ _ Carla. Come on, give it a try. What have you got to lose?
Joe: About _ _ _ _ _ _ !

Discuss your answers with a partner.

Activity 4

Watch the video and answer your teacher's questions. (38:03 – 38:31)

Activity 5

Complete the conversation with the words from the list.

| strength | wrong | idea | to meet | problem |
| own | relax | questions | first | exercise |

Rocky: I don't think that's such a great _ _ _ _ _ _ .
Joe: What?
Rocky: It's set for 35 kilos.
Joe: No _ _ _ _ _ _ . It just takes concentration.
Rocky: Is this your _ _ _ _ _ _ time?
Joe: Yeah.
Rocky: Then _ _ _ _ _ _ . Nobody presses 35 kilos the first time out.
Joe: Really?
Rocky: Sure. You have to start slow and build up your _ _ _ _ _ _ .
Joe: Well, you seem to know a lot about _ _ _ _ _ _ .
Rocky: I should. I _ _ _ _ _ _ the gym. Rocky De Nucci.
Joe: Pleased _ _ _ _ _ _ you. Joe Watson. So, maybe you can tell me what I was doing _ _ _ _ _ _ .
Rocky: Sure. Just answer a few _ _ _ _ _ _ and I'll help you set up an exercise program. Alright?

Discuss your answers with a partner.

Now watch the video and check your answers. (38:32 - 39:15)

Activity 6

Complete the conversation with the words from the list.

terrible	worry
girlfriend	stop
exercise	easy
ready	tennis
stupid	check-up
bike	guy

Rocky: When was the last time you did any regular _ _ _ _ _ _, Joe?

Joe: Oh . . . about six months ago. I used to play _ _ _ _ _ _ with my _ _ _ _ _ _, Carla.

Rocky: Why did you _ _ _ _ _ _?

Joe: She met another _ _ _ _ _ _. Some _ _ _ _ _ _ tennis player, I think . . . You know how it is.

Rocky: Yeah, sure . . . I understand. When was your last medical _ _ _ _ _ _, Joe?

Joe: Last month. The doctor said I was in _ _ _ _ _ _ shape.

Rocky: Don't _ _ _ _ _ _. This exercise program will take care of that. Get on the _ _ _ _ _ _ and we'll start.

Rocky: I'm setting it for ten minutes. OK, _ _ _ _ _ _? Start cycling.

Joe: This is _ _ _ _ _ _! Exercise . . . I love it!

Discuss your answers with a partner.

Now watch the video and check your answers. (40:13 – 41:04)

Activity 7

Complete the conversation with the words from the list.

patient	cycling	kidding	regular	exercise	half an hour
sweat	easy	sit-ups	heart	lose (2)	jog

Rocky: Hey, you OK?

Joe: I think I went about 100 kilometers. Look at this _ _ _ _ _ _! Do you think it's good for you?

Rocky: You have to take it _ _ _ _ _ _ at first. Moderate, regular _ _ _ _ _ _. That's the key.

Joe: What do you mean "_ _ _ _ _ _"?

Rocky: At least three times a week.

Joe: You're _ _ _ _ _ _, right?

Rocky: Twenty minutes to _ _ _ _ _ _ every second day.

Joe: I don't think I'll make it.

Rocky: It takes time. You have to be _ _ _ _ _ _.

Joe: That's easy for you to say. You don't have to _ _ _ _ _ _ ten kilos.

Rocky: Listen. Aerobic exercise like cycling will strengthen your _ _ _ _ _ _ and help you _ _ _ _ _ _ weight. If you don't want to use the bike, you can _ _ _ _ _ _ or swim.

Joe: I think _ _ _ _ _ _ is just fine.

Rocky: OK. We'll go over here a little bit and try a few _ _ _ _ _ _.

Discuss your answers with a partner.

Now watch the video and check your answers. (41:29 – 42:14)

Activity 8

Watch the video and answer your teacher's questions. (43:16 – 43:53)

Activity 1

WHO SAID THIS?

Write J for Joe, F for Frankie, R for Rocky and C for Carla.

☐ Come on, Joe, take it easy with the cheesecake.
☐ I started going to the gym last year. I go every day now.
☐ Rocky De Nucci!. What is this guy – a boxer?
☐ You have to start slow and build up your strength.
☐ I used to play tennis with my girlfriend, Carla.
☐ You have to lose some weight.
☐ I think I went about 100 kilometers.
☐ What do you mean, "regular"?
☐ We'll go over here a little bit and try a few sit-ups.
☐ Ready to go, Rocky?

Discuss your answers with a partner.

Activity 2

WHICH LINE COMES NEXT?

Match the sentences in Column A with the replies in Column B.

COLUMN A	COLUMN B
Don't you get any exercise?	Last month. The doctor said I was in terrible shape.
Where do you work out?	I should. I own the gym.
You seem to know a lot about exercise.	No, not since Carla left. I'm busy all the time.
What do you need to know?	Joe! What a surprise!
How much do you weigh?	At least three times a week.
When was your last medical check-up?	Rocky's Gym. Some guy named Rocky De Nucci owns it.
OK, ready? Start cycling.	Yeah, if I don't die first.
What do you mean "regular"?	This is easy! Exercise . . . I love it.
Good work! In a few weeks you'll be doing fifty.	I don't know. Seventy five, maybe eighty kilos.
Carla!	First, I need to know your full name.

Discuss your answers with a partner.

Activity 3

ROLE PLAY

Read through the script silently. Then read out the script in groups of three, one student taking the roles of Frankie and Carla. The script is on page 62. Now role-play the story.

LANGUAGE CHECK

Activity 1

who	how long
what	how often
where	how much
when	how many
	what kind of

🔲🔘 *Discuss your answers with a partner.*

Complete the conversation using question words from the list.

It is three months later. Frankie and Joe meet again for lunch.

Frankie: Joe, you look great! _ _ _ _ _ _ happened?
Joe: I took your advice, Frankie. I work out.
Frankie: Great! _ _ _ _ _ _ ?
Joe: Rocky's Gym.
Frankie: Yeah? I never see you there. _ _ _ _ _ _ do you usually go?
Joe: Lunch hour.
Frankie: _ _ _ _ _ _ do you work out?
Joe: Three times a week.
Frankie: Good for you, Joe! _ _ _ _ _ _ exercises do you do?
Joe: Different kinds. I ride the bike, lift weights, do sit-ups . . .
Frankie: _ _ _ _ _ _ do you ride the bike?
Joe: Usually for twenty or thirty minutes.
Frankie: _ _ _ _ _ _ weight can you lift now?
Joe: Well, I started with twenty-five kilos. I can lift fifty now.
Frankie: What about sit-ups? _ _ _ _ _ _ can you do?
Joe: Forty. Look at this stomach!
Frankie: Fantastic! _ _ _ _ _ _ set up your exercise program?
Joe: Rocky.
Frankie: Rocky? Isn't he Carla's boyfriend now?
Joe: Yeah, but it doesn't matter. I have a new girlfriend.
Frankie: _ _ _ _ _ _ is she?
Joe: Rosie De Nucci.
Frankie: Rosie De Nucci? You mean . . .
Joe: Yes. My new girlfriend is Rocky's sister.

Activity 2

🔲🔘 *Discuss your answers with a partner.*

Fill in the blanks with the correct form of the verb.

Joe hurt his shoulder lifting weights. He also injured his foot jogging. He went to see Dr. Pachesky about his injuries.

Doctor: What can I _ _ _ _ _ _ (do) for you, Mr. Watson?
Joe: Well, I _ _ _ _ _ _ (hurt) my shoulder and my foot.
Doctor: How _ _ _ _ _ _ you _ _ _ _ _ _ (hurt) yourself?
Joe: Well, I _ _ _ _ _ _ (hurt) my shoulder while I _ _ _ _ _ _ (lift) weights. I _ _ _ _ _ _ (lift) 60 kilos when I _ _ _ _ _ _ (feel) a sharp pain in my shoulder.
Doctor: Where _ _ _ _ _ _ it _ _ _ _ _ _ (hurt)? Right here? (*The doctor touches his shoulder.*)
Joe: Ouch! Yeah, there.
Doctor: Well, you have to be more careful when you _ _ _ _ _ _ (exercise). Now what about your foot?
Joe: Well, I _ _ _ _ _ _ (go) jogging the day before yesterday. I _ _ _ _ _ _ (jog) in the park, but I _ _ _ _ _ _ (not, look) where I _ _ _ _ _ _ (go). Suddenly I _ _ _ _ _ _ (step) on a banana peel. I _ _ _ _ _ _ (fall) and _ _ _ _ _ _ (hurt) my foot. Right here.
Doctor: Yes, I _ _ _ _ _ _ (see).
Joe: So, Doctor, _ _ _ _ _ _ I _ _ _ _ _ _ (be) OK by tomorrow? I have to _ _ _ _ _ _ (work out).
Doctor: No, Mr. Watson, you _ _ _ _ _ _ (not, be) OK by tomorrow. In fact, you _ _ _ _ _ _ (not, be) OK for at least two weeks.
Joe: _ _ _ _ _ _ you _ _ _ _ _ _ (tell) me not to exercise for two weeks?
Doctor: Yes, Mr. Watson, I am . . . Why _ _ _ _ _ _ you _ _ _ _ _ _ (smile)?
Joe: Because I _ _ _ _ _ _ (not, like) to exercise! In fact, I _ _ _ _ _ _ (hate) it!

READING RETELL

Read Text A and answer the questions.

1 When and where was "Jackrabbit" Johanssen born?

2 When did he come to Canada?

3 What was his occupation?

4 Where did his company send him?

5 Why did the Indians give him the name "Jackrabbit"?

6 Why did he love Canada?

7 Where did he move with his family in 1928?

8 Did they live in a big house?

9 Did they have a car, telephone and electricity?

10 How did "Jackrabbit" go from place to place?

11 Did other people become interested in skiing?

12 What did he decide to make?

13 What did he still do at the age of 100?

14 How old was Jackrabbit when he died?

🔊 **Check your answers with a partner.**

Retell your story to a student with Text B.

TEXT A   Jackrabbit Johanssen

Herman "Jackrabbit" Johanssen was the man who brought cross-country skiing to Canada. He was born in Oslo, Norway on June 15, 1875. In 1902 he came to Canada to work for the railroad. He was an engineer. His company sent him to the north woods of Ontario. He lived with the Cree Indians. There were no roads and no cars. He travelled on skis. The Indians watched the way he skied. He looked like a rabbit, jumping quickly from place to place. They gave him the name "Jackrabbit".

Jackrabbit loved Canada. The country was beautiful – there were woods, lakes and rivers. He liked the cold weather. In 1928 he moved to the mountains north of Montreal with his family. There were few people in that area. They lived in a small house in the woods. They had no car, no telephone and no electricity. It was hard but they learned to do things for themselves.

The mountains were a perfect place to ski. Jackrabbit used skis to go from place to place. Other people became interested and wanted Jackrabbit to teach them how to ski. Jackrabbit decided to make a ski trail. It was the first cross-country ski trail in Canada. It was 125 kilometers long and took three years to make. Today this trail is one of the best in the world.

Jackrabbit believed that skiing kept him young. He lived a long and healthy life. At the age of 100 he still skied every day. He enjoyed teaching young people. He started many young people's ski clubs. He taught them how to ski and went with them on trips. When he died at the age of 111, many of the young people said that Jackrabbit not only showed them how to ski, but also how to live.

Read Text B and answer the questions.

1 Who is Jackie Joyner-Kersee?

2 What sports competition does she compete in?

3 When and where was Jackie born?

4 What information is given about her family?

5 What were her main interests as a young girl?

6 When did she run her first race? Did she win?

7 Who did she beat when she was 12?

8 When she was 14, what did she watch on television?

9 What did she want to compete in?

10 What did Jackie win at 18?

11 Who was Robert Kersee?

12 What happened a few years later?

13 What did Jackie win at the Los Angeles Olympic Games?

14 What did she do in 1986?

15 What did she win at the Seoul Olympics?

🔘🔘 **Check your answers with a partner.**

Retell your story to a student with Text A.

TEXT B **Jackie Joyner-Kersee**

Jackie Joyner-Kersee is the greatest female athlete in the world. She competes in the most difficult sports competition for women - the heptathlon. The heptathlon is difficult because there are seven different events: the 100-meter hurdles, shot put, javelin, long jump, high jump, 200-meter run and 800-meter run.

Jackie was born in East St. Louis, Illinois on March 3, 1962. East St. Louis is a town with a lot of poor people and a lot of crime. When Jackie was born, her mother was only 16 and her father, only 17. They had four children. The family was poor. Sometimes they were too poor to pay the heating bill. But Jackie's parents wanted their children to stay in school and get a good education.

As a young girl, Jackie's main interests were school and sports. She ran her first race when she was nine. She finished last. But soon she was winning all her races. She could beat all the boys in the neighbourhood. When she was 12, she even beat her older brother in a race in front of his friends. When she was 14, Jackie watched the Montreal Olympic Games on television. She decided that she wanted to compete in the Olympics.

At 18, Jackie won a basketball scholarship to the University of California at Los Angeles. Robert Kersee was a young coach at the university. He thought she could be an Olympic champion. He became her coach and she began to train for the heptathlon. She trained hard almost every day. Jackie and her coach became friends. Then they fell in love. A few years later they got married.

At the Los Angeles Olympic Games in 1984 Jackie didn't win a gold medal. She won only a silver. She was very disappointed, but she continued to train even harder. In 1986 she set a world record in the heptathlon. Then she broke her record three times in two years. In 1988 at the Seoul Olympics she won the gold medal in her favourite event, the long jump. She also won the gold medal in the heptathlon and set a new world record.

Functions

Now you can:

Request/Give information	How old are you? Twenty-nine. How tall are you? I'm 1 meter 85 cm. How much do you weigh? I don't know. 75, maybe 80 kilos.
Give instructions	Get on the bike. Start cycling. Keep your knees bent.
Express obligation and necessity	You have to lose some weight. You have to be patient.
Give opinions	You don't look so good. This is easy. I think cycling is just fine. You seem to know a lot about exercise. I don't think that's going to happen.
Give encouragement	Good work. Don't worry. It takes time.

Structures

Simple past	I started going to the gym last year. She met another guy.
Interrogative:	Why did you stop? When did you become Mr. Fitness?
Future with 'will'	This exercise program will take care of that. Cycling will strengthen your heart.
'used to' + infinitive	I used to play tennis. He used to be some kind of tennis player.
'have to' + infinitive	You have to lose some weight. You have to be patient.
Time expressions	20 minutes half an hour every day three times a week in a few weeks last month last year
Imperative	Start cycling. Give it a try.
Question words	Where do you work out? What do you need to know? What do you mean? How old are you? How tall are you? How much do you weigh? When was your last medical check-up? When was the last time you did any regular exercise? Why did you stop?

Words and expressions

gym	to work out	body	easy	You're kidding, right?
aerobic exercise	to lose weight	stomach		Your turn.
program	to swim	knees	Take it easy!	Wait a minute!
shape	to jog	head	Lunch is on me.	That's right.
strength	to strengthen	hands	Come on, give it a try.	
sweat	(the heart)	muscle	No problem.	
bike	to build up		Really?	
sit-ups	(muscles)	awful	Sure.	
weight	to set	terrible	Pleased to meet you.	
boxer	to press	regular	Let's check it out.	
tennis player	(weights)	moderate	Hey, you OK?	

1 The customer is always right

Salesclerk: May I help you with anything?

Customer: Ah no, not right now, thank you. I'm just looking.

Salesclerk: May I take your . . . your coat and bag?

Customer: Pretty big bag, eh? Thank you very much. I'm a little warm in this. I'm not very well-dressed, am I?

Salesclerk Well, you are here to buy new clothes, aren't you?

Customer: That's right . . . I'm looking for a dress.

Salesclerk: What size do you take?

Customer: Size 10.

Salesclerk: I think a size 12 dress would fit you perfectly. Follow me, please. (*She shows the customer the pink dress.*) This is our latest style. Isn't it beautiful?

Customer: I don't really like the color . . . Do you have something in blue?

Salesclerk: No. This dress only comes in pink. Pink is the new winter color.

Customer: Here's one in blue. I love the belt.

Salesclerk: Yes, it's nice, but it is last year's style.

Customer: Maybe I can try them both on?

Salesclerk: Certainly, madam.

Customer: Thank you.

Salesclerk: Would you like to look at the skirts?

Customer: Sure, what do you have? This is beautiful. Does it come in brown?

Salesclerk: No . . . only black.

Customer: (*Taking another skirt*) Oh, I like this one . . . I like the buttons.

Salesclerk: That is a size 8, madam. (*She shows the customer another skirt.*) This is a size 12. Isn't it a lovely design?

Customer: Oh, I like this one in green.

Salesclerk: You can try them both on.

Customer: Hey, just a minute, please. I'd like to try on one of these suits. I like this red one. It's only 150 dollars. You don't like it?

Salesclerk: I think you'd look much better in this black one.

Customer: How much does it cost?

Salesclerk: It was 550, but it's been reduced to 350 dollars.

Customer: Three hundred and fifty dollars is a lot of money! It's more expensive than this one.

Salesclerk: Believe me, madam, it's worth the extra money. Just look at the material . . . and the style.

Customer: Well, maybe I could . . .

Salesclerk: . . . try them both on? Yes, of course. Would you like a blouse?

Customer: What do you have? (*The customer takes a grey blouse. The salesclerk takes a white blouse.*)

Salesclerk: Follow me, please. (*The customer tries on the blue dress.*)

Customer: Ta da! (*Looking in the mirror*) Ah, I love it. It's so comfortable. You don't like it.

Salesclerk: Well, it is last year's style. Why don't you try on the pink one I showed you? (*The customer tries on the pink dress.*) Wonderful! It's beautiful on you.

Customer: Yes, but the shoulders are too tight, and it's too long.

Salesclerk: Well, we can shorten it. Or you can wear it with a belt. And this scarf is perfect! . . .You do like the dress, don't you?

Customer: Yes . . .

Salesclerk: Well, then I think you should buy it. Now, why don't you try on the skirts?

(*The customer tries on the green skirt, the skirt with a design, and finally the red suit.*)

Customer: Now, this looks good, doesn't it?

Salesclerk: Yes, it's nice. But the color . . .

Customer: I thought I looked good in red.

Salesclerk: Well, it's up to you, but I really think that you should . . .

Customer: . . . try on the black suit. (*The customer tries on the black suit.*) It's too big.

Salesclerk: We can take it in.

Customer: Three hundred and fifty dollars is a lot of money.

Salesclerk: It is the latest style.

Customer: I know that, but . . .

Salesclerk: Well, it is your decision.

Customer: You're right. It is my decision.

Salesclerk: You won't regret it, madam.

Customer: No, I won't regret it. (*The salesclerk folds the black suit, pink dress and skirt with a design. The customer comes out of the changing room.*)

Salesclerk: You're going to love these clothes. The dress is beautiful, and the suit is perfect for you. (*The customer goes to the door and leaves the store.*) Madam . . . madam . . . (*She looks around and walks towards the door.*) . . . Hello. Madam! Wait! What about your clothes?

2 Doctor knows best

Rec: The doctor will see you now. (*It is 4:00 p.m. John Hunter stands at the receptionist's desk in a doctor's office. He is smoking a cigarette.*)

Mr. Hunter: Excuse me. I'm John Hunter. I have an appointment with Dr. Pachesky.

Rec: Oh yes, Mr. Hunter. I'll need your medical insurance card. (*Mr. Hunter hands her the card.*)

Rec: Thank you. If you'd just take a seat over there, I'll call you when the doctor is ready. And, Mr. Hunter! This is a "No Smoking" area.

Mr. Hunter: Oh, gee . . . Uh, do you have an ashtray?

Rec: No Mr. Hunter. I don't smoke. (*Mr. Hunter takes a seat in the waiting room. Then he gets up, goes over by a window and lights up a cigarette.*)

Rec: Mr. Hunter! The doctor will see you now. (*Mr. Hunter tries to hide the cigarette.*)

Mr. Hunter: Ah, nice view.

Rec: And I'll take that cigarette! Follow me, please.

(*In the doctor's office*)

Doctor: Sorry to keep you waiting, Mr. Hunter.

Mr. Hunter: That's OK. (*He looks at his watch.*) It's only been about a half an hour.

Doctor: So, what can I do for you today?

Mr. Hunter: Well, I'm a little worried about my heart.

Doctor: Oh really? Well why are you so worried?

Mr. Hunter: Yesterday, when I was at work, I got a pain, ah . . . right here. (*He points to his left side.*)

Doctor: Could you describe it to me?

Mr. Hunter: Well, it started out as a dull ache and then it turned into a sharp pain. It really hurt.

Doctor: Anything else?

Mr. Hunter: Yeah, I felt dizzy and I could hardly breathe. I had to sit down and rest for fifteen minutes.

Doctor: Hmm-mm.

Mr. Hunter: Do you think it's my heart?

Doctor: I'm not sure, but I would like to ask you a few more questions. How old are you?

Mr. Hunter: About forty-five.

Doctor: Do you smoke?

Mr. Hunter: Yeah.

Doctor: How much?

Mr. Hunter: A pack a day . . . sometimes two.

Doctor: How long have you been smoking?

Mr. Hunter: Oh, I don't know. Twenty years, maybe longer.

Doctor: Twenty years is a long time, a long time.

Mr. Hunter: I know. But I like to smoke. It relaxes me.

Doctor: Oh, I understand, I understand. But it's bad for your health. Do you drink a lot of coffee, too?

Mr. Hunter: Yeah, but I've cut down a lot lately.

Doctor: How many cups a day?

Mr. Hunter: Oh, . . . eight or nine.

Doctor: Two or three cups a day is all you should drink. It's bad for the heart.

Mr. Hunter: But I need coffee. I'm a journalist. I work long hours.

Doctor: I know what you mean . . . Well, I think I have to examine you. Would you take off your shirt, please, and go sit on the examining table. *(Mr. Hunter is sitting on the examining table.)*

Doctor: All right. We're just going to check your lungs now. All right, now breathe in. No, no, no. Not like that. Deeper. Like this. *(The doctor takes a deep breath and starts to cough.)*

Doctor: Excuse me, Mr. Hunter. I'm . . . I'm sorry about that. All right, breathe in . . . out . . .

Mr. Hunter: Is it OK?

Doctor: Yes, I'm surprised. It's excellent. Well, Mr. Hunter, you seem to be in good health. but I'd like to order a few tests just to make sure.

Mr. Hunter: Then there is something wrong.

Doctor: No, no, no. There's nothing to worry about. But if you want to stay in good health, I would quit smoking . . . and cut down on coffee, too.

Mr. Hunter: Yeah, I'll try.

Doctor: Oh, . . . and make another appointment on your way out. If there's anything you need, just call. I'll be happy to help.

Mr. Hunter: Right . . . Thanks a lot. *(Mr Hunter puts on his shirt and reaches for a cigarette. He looks at the packet, then throws it in the garbage.)*

(Mr. Hunter is standing at the receptionist's desk.)

Mr. Hunter: So, I just threw the whole pack in the garbage. This time I really think I'm going to quit.

Rec: That's great, Mr. Hunter. We'll see you tomorrow at 4:30 then? *(As she talks, the doctor comes around the corner, a cigarette in his mouth.)*

Doctor: *(To receptionist)* Julie, do we have any fresh coffee? Mr. Hunter! You're still here?

Mr. Hunter: You smoke!

Doctor: What? *(He looks at his cigarette.)* Oh, this! Well . . . well, you're a smoker. You understand how it is, Mr. Hunter. You smoke.

Mr. Hunter: Not anymore. I just quit. *(To receptionist)* How many cups of coffee does he drink?

Rec: About ten cups a day.

Mr. Hunter: Ten cups! Doesn't he know that that's bad for his heart?

Doctor: Ah, but I work long hours . . . I need coffee. *(He starts to cough.)*

Mr. Hunter: And that cough! I really

think he should quit smoking, don't you?

Doctor: OK. OK, you're right. *(He puts out the cigarette.)*

Mr. Hunter: The whole pack, please. *(The doctor gives the pack to Mr. Hunter.)*

Mr. Hunter: Oh, and doctor? If you need anything else, just call. I'll be happy to help.

3 Cooking with Arlene

(Dennis Johnson is talking on the phone in his office.)

Dennis: Yeah, it looks great. I'd just like to know where Arlene is. *(He hangs up. The phone rings again.)*

Dennis: Hello, Arlene! Where are you? . . . the hospital? But Arlene, the show starts in 20 minutes . . . What do you mean, you can't do the show? Who's going to do it? Me? . . . Well, yeah, I can cook, but . . . Arlene, I can't . . . Hello. Hello, Arlene? *(He hangs up the phone. Janet drops a paper on his desk.)*

Janet: Here's today's script, Dennis.

Dennis: *(On the phone)* Hello, boss, it's Dennis . . . Yeah, we have a big problem. Arlene can't do the show . . . I should do it? Boss, I can't cook on TV. Not in front of all those people . . . Yeah, but, Mr. Black!! . . . I can't . . . Hello. Hello . . .

(Dennis hangs up the phone.)

Dennis: I am not doing that show!

(Dennis in the kitchen)

Dennis: Hello and welcome to "Cooking with Arlene". . . That's no good . . . Hello, my name is Dennis Johnson and welcome to "Cooking with Arlene".

(Janet is speaking on the phone.)

Janet: Yeah, well, I'm sorry to hear that, Arlene. Yeah, I'll tell him after the show, OK . . . yeah . . . All the best . . . OK . . . Yeah, bye.

Dennis: *(Practicing)* Hi, I'm Dennis Johnson and this is "Cooking with Arlene". Oh, I can't do this!

Janet: OK, Dennis, you're on in five seconds.

Dennis: No, Janet . . . I'm not ready! I'm not ready!

Janet: And five . . . four . . . three . . .

Dennis: Janet, stop! Stop! Just a second . . . I can't . . . stop, I can't. I can't . . .

Janet: . . . two . . . one . . . and you're on.

(Dennis looks at the camera, but does not move.)

Janet: *(Whispering)* Dennis, Dennis, the introduction!

Dennis: The introduction? Oh, the introduction! Yes . . . Hi . . . and welcome to "Cooking with Arlene". My name is Dennis Johnson, so

today we'll be "Cooking with Dennis" . . . My name is Dennis . . .

Janet: *(Whispering)* The recipe!

Dennis: OK . . . So, well, we're here to cook, so let's cook, huh? What are we cooking, Janet?

Janet: Spanish omelets.

Dennis: Did you hear that, folks? Today we're cooking Spanish omelets. I love omelets, don't you? And, of course, as we all know, the main ingredients in omelets are eggs. *(He looks around.)* . . . Eggs . . . little round white things, like this *(Makes a circle with his fingers)* . . . kind of round and . . . white . . .

Janet: *(Whispering)* On the counter... behind you!

(Dennis gets the eggs.)

Dennis: Our eggs. Now then, we have our eggs and the recipe calls for . . . four eggs . . . one, two, three, and *(He drops the fourth egg on the counter.)* . . . four . . . We take our three eggs and break them into the bowl. And, of course, omelets are good for you . . . and they're fun to eat . . . and not only that, but they're really easy to make. And . . . once we have our three eggs in the bowl, we . . . add a little milk . . . *(Whispering)* Where's the milk, Janet?

Janet: In the fridge – behind you!

Dennis: Fridge. It's always a good idea to keep your milk in the fridge.

(He gets the milk and puts a little in the bowl.)

Dennis: OK. So, we add a little milk and then we beat the whole thing together . . . Now, you can use one of these hand beaters or you can use one of these electric beaters like I'm going to use.

(He puts the beater into the bowl and turns it on high.)

Dennis: Always remember to keep the beater on low . . . You know, I love to cook . . . My Mom, when I was a little guy, always used to tell me, when you're cooking never, ever hurry . . .

(Janet tells him to hurry.)

Dennis: . . . or you make mistakes. Once we've got that done, we're ready to add our other ingredients. You'll need an onion, a green pepper, a tomato, and some salt and pepper, and some oil for the frying pan *(He looks around.)* . . . The frying pan, Janet? . . .

Janet: The right drawer.

(Dennis goes to the left drawer.)

Janet: Not the left – the right!

(Dennis holds up the pan.)

Dennis: Our pan. OK, now what we do is, we add a little oil to the pan . . . just a little at the bottom here. There we go. And we put that on medium heat.

(He turns the stove on high without looking.)

Dennis: Now, next, we chop up our onion. Always remember when you're chopping onions to breathe through your mouth. Otherwise, if you breathe through your nose . . . like that . . . you may start . . . to cry . . .

Janet: Dennis . . . Dennis . . . the pan!

Dennis: And watch your pan! We wouldn't want to burn our onions, would we? *(He takes the onions and adds them to the frying pan.)*

Dennis: OK. We add our onions . . . and we get ready to add our other ingredients. *(Dennis picks up the green pepper and the knife.)* Next, we quickly chop a green pepper. You know, I like to sing when I cook at home. Perfect! What a great idea! Why don't we all sing? "When the moon hits your eyes like a big pizza pie, that's amore! When you walk down the street any chance that you meet, that's amore . . ."

Janet: Dennis! *(She makes a sign to him to hurry.)*

Dennis: Yeah, OK. So, once you've got all that done, you add that mixture to your onions . . . There we go . . . *(Smells)* Mmmmmm! . . . OK, now we let that simmer for three minutes.

Janet: You have one minute left, Dennis.

Dennis: *(Quickly adding the eggs to the pan)* Er . . . I think those three minutes are up, don't you? OK. And, we now get ready to add our eggs. Oh, yeah! Here we go. A little salt and pepper . . . and we're cooking!

Janet: Forty seconds.

Dennis: Er . . . OK, so you flip your omelet.

Janet: Thirty seconds.

Dennis: Once it's all cooked, you dish it up on the plate.

(He puts the omelet on the plate.)

Janet: Fifteen seconds.

Dennis: Ah . . . and oh, and add a little parsley and tomato for colour . . . And doesn't that look good? Don't forget to write for today's recipe.

Janet: That's it, folks!

Dennis: Thank goodness that's over!

Janet: It's OK, Dennis. The first time is always the hardest. You'll get better.

Dennis: What do you mean, "I'll get better"?

Janet: Arlene called again. She's going to be in the hospital for a month. Looks like you'll be doing three more shows, Dennis.

(She walks away laughing.)

Dennis: Oh, no! . . . Janet . . . wait . . . I . . . can't . . . Janet . . . no . . . Janet, wait . . . I can't . . . Janet . . .

4 Vacation for two?

Helen: Come on, George.

George: No. We went skiing last year.

Helen: But you love to ski.

George: You love to ski, I love to suntan.

Helen: And you need the exercise.

George: I'm not getting fat and I'm not going skiing.

Helen: Fine. I'll go alone.

George: Helen!

Helen: I'm serious, George. If you don't want to come, I will go by myself.

George: Don't be silly.

Helen: I'm not being silly!

George: Helen, please, you're shouting.

Helen: I'm not shouting.

(The travel agent can't take another minute of this.)

Agent: Excuse me!

Helen & George: What?

Agent: Can I help you?

George: I doubt it.

Helen: We want to book our winter vacation.

George: Your vacation, you mean.

Helen: George. Why are you being so difficult?

Agent: Please, have a seat. I'm sure I can help.

Agent: OK. Now, where is it you'd like to go?

Helen: I would like to go skiing.

Agent: Great. There's lots of beautiful places to go. Let's see. You could go to the Laurentians *(She takes some brochures.)* . . . or maybe Vermont, Colorado, Montana . . .

George: *(Interrupting)* Florida.

Agent: Florida?

George: That's right. I want the hot sun and sandy beaches.

Agent: OK, there's lots of places you can get that, too *(Again, she reaches for brochures.)* . . . Have you thought of . . . Mexico or maybe the Caribbean?

Helen: Beaches are . . . so boring.

George: *(To Helen)* So is skiing, Helen. Look! I look at the snow eight months a year. I don't want to see it on my two weeks off.

Helen: *(To the agent)* No, he wants to lay on the beach and bake in the hot sun!

George: What's wrong with that?

Agent: Could I ask you a question? Have you thought of taking separate vacations?

George: You mean go alone . . . to different places?

Agent: Sure. A lot of married couples do it.

George: Yeah, but they don't stay married for long.

Agent: Actually, it can be really good

to take a vacation alone sometimes. But I tell you what, you take a look at the brochures for a couple of minutes . . . five, ten minutes . . . and we can make the bookings a little later on. *(She gets up.)* I have a phone call to make right now, if you'll excuse me.

(The travel agent makes the phone call and returns.)

Agent: So, have you made your decision?

George: A lot of these places are too expensive, but this one in Mexico looks good.

Helen: I like the ski resort in Colorado.

(The agent turns to the computer.)

Agent: OK. Can I get your dates, please?

Helen: Sure. February 10th to the 24th. Forget Valentine's Day.

Agent: *(Turning back to them)* You're in luck. I have openings on those dates for both places. Do you want to book them?

George: Yeah, I guess so.

Agent: *(To George)* OK. Now, will you be needing to rent a car while you're there?

George: Well, it says here in the brochure that the hotel provides free transportation from the airport and it's right on the beach.

Agent: *(To Helen)* How about you?

Helen: No . . . it appears that the ski resort is right on the mountain.

Agent: OK. Then we're ready. *(To Helen)* Can I start with you? Can I get your full name, please?

Helen: George and Helen Kowalski . . . Helen Kowalski. K-O-W-A-L-S-K-I.

Agent: OK. Helen, you will be leaving on Flight 145 to Boulder, Colorado, on Saturday, February 10th . . . returning on Flight 129 on Sunday, February 24th. I'll have your ticket . . .

George: *(He turns to Helen.)* Hold it, I don't want to go to Acapulco by myself. If it's that important to you, we'll go skiing. I mean . . . the sun shines in the mountains, too, right?

Helen: *(Smiling)* No, George. I was wrong. Look, we went skiing last year. We should do what you want to do this year.

George: I don't mind skiing really.

Helen: No. I want to go to Mexico.

George: Are you sure?

Helen: *(Louder and impatient)* Yes, I'm sure.

George: Well, we don't have to go if you don't want to.

Helen: *(Loudly)* I want to go.

George: Well, you don't have to get mad.

Helen: I'm not getting mad.

Agent: Excuse me! *(She answers the phone.)* Hello. Oh, yes, hi. Yes. Great! OK, can you give me the details. Uh-huh. OK. Yeah, February

10th to the 24th. Yeah, that's perfect. OK, I'll call you right back. Thanks a lot. 'Bye 'bye.

(She hangs up the phone and George immediately speaks.)

George: Maybe we should finish those separate bookings.

Agent: Listen, you two. I don't think you really want to go on separate vacations, do you?

(George looks at Helen and both of them smile and start to laugh.)

Agent: I've got another suggestion. I just called the Hawaiian travel bureau and I can get a package to the island that includes four days of skiing at Mount Mauna Kea. What do you think?

Helen: Oh, it sounds perfect!

George: Yeah, but is it expensive?

Agent: No more expensive than paying for separate vacations.

Helen: *(Smiling at George)* Is the hotel on the beach?

Agent: It sure is. There's swimming and water skiing and sailing . . .

George: Scuba diving?

Agent: Sure. They have scuba diving lessons, too.

Helen: Oh, it sounds great. We'll take it.

Agent: Terrific! Listen, your tickets will be ready in about a week's time.

George: Thanks very much. *(He shakes hands.)*

Helen: Yeah, you've been a big help. *(She shakes hands with the travel agent.)*

Agent: My pleasure. Listen, I hope you have a wonderful vacation.

Helen & George: Oh, we will.

Agent: 'Bye now.

Helen: 'Bye.

Agent: *(Shaking her head)* Thanks, Charlie. Listen, I'm telling you, sometimes I think I should be doing this full time . . .

(Charlie looks at her with a questioning look. After all, she's already a full-time travel agent.)

Agent: Marriage counselling . . . it probably pays better, too, don't you think? *(Charlie hands her some papers.)* Thanks a lot.

5 Maxie's revenge

Desmond: OK, get in here . . . OK, empty your pockets and sit down!

Desmond: So, your name is William Lukeman, right?

Maxie: Yeah.

Desmond: *(Reading from a card in one of the wallets)* Age 49, brown hair, brown eyes, 1 metre 55, 70 kilos, taxi driver, married.

(Desmond looks through the second wallet and pulls out some cards.)

Desmond: Oh, this is interesting. Your name is also George Taylor.

Maxie: Sure.

Desmond: George Taylor, age 34, brown hair, blue eyes, 1 metre 74, 80 kilos, lawyer, married.

(Desmond repeats the action with a third wallet.)

Desmond: And look at this. Your name is also Ken Cooper.

Maxie: Why not? It's a nice name.

Desmond: Ken Cooper. Age 22, blond hair, blue eyes, 1 metre 68, 80 kilos, car mechanic and single. So, let's see. Your name is William Lukeman. Your name is George Taylor. Your name is also Ken Cooper.

Maxie: Well, I like a lot of variety in my life.

Desmond: You're 49, 22 and 34. You're single and you're married. You're a taxi driver, a lawyer and a mechanic.

Maxie: I could never hang onto a job.

Desmond: So. *Who* are you?

Maxie: You're the detective. You find out.

Malloy: Answer the question.

Desmond: It's OK, Malloy. We'll get his fingerprints. We'll find out who he is.

Malloy: Come on. Give us an answer.

(Maxie still doesn't answer.)

Desmond: OK, Malloy, take him to the cell. Maybe he'll remember who he is . . . after a few days.

Maxie: OK! OK! My name is Maxie Gardiner.

Desmond: Maxie Gardiner. We'll check that name out. OK. Get him out of here.

(Malloy takes Maxie by the arm.)

Malloy: Let's go, Maxie.

(Later in the day)

Desmond: OK, Malloy, bring him in.

(Malloy brings Maxie in.)

Desmond: Ah, so, your name really is Maxie Gardiner. *(reading from paper)* Maxwell Gardiner, age 40, 1 metre 65, 75 kilos, married and divorced twice, no fixed address. First arrest was in 1962. Total of five arrests in all. Eleven years in jail. Congratulations, Maxie, you're well-known. You're the number one pickpocket in the country.

Maxie: That's right, cop. I'm the best.

Desmond: Well, you made one big mistake. You came to Montreal and met us. Bring in Mrs. Colombo.

(Malloy goes to the door and calls in Mrs. Colombo.)

Malloy: Mrs. Colombo.

(Mrs. Colombo walks in.)

Desmond: Is this the man, Mrs. Colombo? Take your time. Look carefully.

Mrs. C.: I don't have to take my time, young man. That's him. I'm sure it's him. That's the thief.

Desmond: Are you absolutely sure?

Mrs. C.: Yes, I am. I'm absolutely sure. That's the man.

Desmond: Thank you, Mrs. Colombo. Take him away.

(Malloy leads Maxie away.)

Malloy: Let's go.

Desmond: Thank you, Mrs. Colombo. But, tell me, why did you have a mousetrap in your purse?

Mrs. C.: Officer, I was robbed last year. A man stole my wallet right out of my bag. It won't happen again. *(She opens her purse and takes out the mousetrap.)*

Desmond: That's for sure, Mrs. Colombo. Thanks again.

Mrs. C.: Not at all. It's my pleasure.

(Later in the day. Maxie is back in the room.)

Malloy: Well, Maxie, you're finished. We were just too smart for you.

Maxie: Smart, hah! You were just lucky! Crazy old woman! *(Looks at his bandaged finger.)* A mousetrap in her purse!

Malloy: Well, too bad for you, Maxie boy. You're going to jail for a nice, long vacation. And we're going to Joe's Steak House for dinner. *(Grabs Maxie's arm)*

(He laughs as he leads Maxie away.)

(Joe's Steak House – supper-time)

Desmond: Great steak, Malloy. *(Lights up a cigarette)* That was good work today.

Malloy: Yeah.

Desmond: I wonder what our friend Maxie is having for supper tonight.

Malloy: Bread and water, I hope. *(They both laugh.)* Waitress! Waitress! The bill, please.

Desmond: It's a good restaurant here.

Malloy: Yeah.

(The waitress brings the bill.)

Malloy: Thank you.

Desmond: How much is it?

Malloy: Forty-two dollars.

Desmond: OK, we'll pay it and leave.

(Malloy reaches for his wallet. It's not there. He looks in his other pockets. His wallet is gone.)

Malloy: My wallet! I can't find my wallet!

(Malloy checks his pockets again.)

Malloy: I probably left it at the station. Can you pay?

Desmond: No problem.

(Desmond reaches for his wallet. It's not there.)

Desmond: Oh no!!

Malloy: Ah come on!

Desmond: *(He searches all his pockets.)* What's happening? What's going on? . . . Hey, what's this? *(He pulls a note from his pocket, reads it and smiles.)*

Malloy: What does the note say?

Desmond: *(Reading the note)* "I hope you boys like washing dishes. Your friend... Maxie."
(They look at each other, surprised and shocked.)
Malloy: Oh, that sneaky little creep!

6 Getting in shape

(In a restaurant. Lunchtime. Joe is having lunch with Frankie.)
Frankie: The bill, please. Come on, Joe, take it easy with the cheesecake.
Joe: I'm telling you, Frankie. I feel awful.
Frankie: Well, you don't look so good either.
Joe: Thank you.
Frankie: Don't you get any exercise?
Joe: No, not since Carla left. I'm busy all the time. I work all day.
Frankie: You eat, don't you?
Joe: Yeah, so?
Frankie: So if you've got the time to eat, you've got the time to exercise.
Joe: Since when did you become Mr. Fitness?
Frankie: Hey, I started going to the gym last year. I go every day now.
Joe: Every day?
Frankie: Uh-huh. Come on. Lunch is on me.
Joe: Frankie. Frankie, I'm not finished my cheesecake. Where do you work out?
Frankie: Rocky's Gym. Some guy named Rocky De Nucci owns it.
Joe: Rocky De Nucci! What is this guy – a boxer?
Frankie: Nah! I think he used to be some kind of tennis player.
Joe: Oh no, not another tennis player!
Frankie: Will you forget about Carla? Come on, give it a try. What have you got to lose?
Joe: About ten kilos!

(At Rocky's Gym. People are working out with weights. Joe lies on a bench and tries to lift a weight. He has a hard time.)
Rocky: I don't think that's such a great idea.
Joe: What?
Rocky: It's set for 35 kilos.
Joe: No problem. It just takes concentration.
Rocky: Is this your first time?
Joe: Yeah.
Rocky: Then relax. Nobody presses 35 kilos the first time out.
Joe: Really?
Rocky: Sure. You have to start slow and build up your strength.
Joe: Well, you seem to know a lot about exercise.
Rocky: I should. I own the gym. Rocky De Nucci.

Joe: Pleased to meet you. Joe Watson. So, maybe you can tell me what I was doing wrong.
Rocky: Sure. Just answer a few questions and I'll help you set up an exercise program. Alright?
Joe: OK, what do you need to know?
Rocky: First, I need to know your full name.
Joe: Joseph Allan Watson.
Rocky: How old are you, Joe?
Joe: Twenty-nine.
Rocky: And how tall are you?
Joe: 1 meter 85.
Rocky: Now for that special question . . . How much do you weigh?
Joe: Oh, I don't know. Seventy-five . . . maybe eighty kilos.
Rocky: Come on, let's check it out. The scales are over here.
(Joe gets on the scales and Rocky looks at the results.)
It's too much, Joe.
Joe: Rocky, I still have my shoes on.
Rocky: You have to lose some weight. At least . . . ten kilos.
Joe: That much? I thought about ten.
Rocky: When was the last time you did any regular exercise, Joe?
Joe: Oh . . . about six months ago. I used to play tennis with my girlfriend, Carla.
Rocky: Why did you stop?
Joe: She met another guy. Some stupid tennis player, I think . . . You know how it is.
Rocky: Yeah, sure . . . I understand. When was your last medical check-up, Joe?
Joe: Last month. The doctor said I was in terrible shape.
Rocky: Don't worry. This exercise program will take care of that. Get on the bike and we'll start.
(Joe gets on the bike.)
Rocky: I'm setting it for ten minutes. OK, ready? Start cycling.
Joe: This is easy! Exercise . . . I love it!

(Ten minutes later.)
Rocky: Hey, you OK?
Joe: I think I went about 100 kilometres. Look at this sweat! Do you think it's good for you?
Rocky: You have to take it easy at first. Moderate, regular exercise. That's the key.
Joe: What do you mean "regular"?
Rocky: At least three times a week.
Joe: You're kidding, right?
Rocky: Twenty minutes to half an hour every second day.
Joe: I don't think I'll make it.
Rocky: It takes time. You have to be patient.
Joe: That's easy for you to say. You don't have to lose 10 kilos.
Rocky: Listen. Aerobic exercise like cycling will strengthen your heart and help you lose weight. If you

don't want to use the bike, you can jog or swim.
Joe: I think cycling is just fine.
Rocky: OK. We'll go over here a little bit and try a few . . . sit-ups.
Joe: Great! That should be a lot of fun!
(They walk over and get ready to do sit-ups. Rocky demonstrates.)
Rocky: Sit-ups are good for your stomach. Keep your knees bent. Hands beside your head and pull up, like this. OK? Your turn.
(Joe starts to do sit-ups.)
Joe: Sit-ups I know I can do. One . . . two . . . three . . .
Rocky: Take it easy!
Joe: Four . . . five . . . six . . . seven . . . eight . . . nine . . . ten!
Rocky: Good work! In a few weeks time you'll be doing fifty!
Joe: Yeah, if I don't die first.
Rocky: Don't worry, you'll live. Come on, we have a lot more to do.
Joe: There's more? Oh!

(Joe is finished exercising. He and Rocky are standing at the front desk.)
Rocky: So how are you doing now?
Joe: Every muscle in my body aches. Thanks.
Rocky: Don't worry. Pain goes away . . . like a broken heart.
Joe: Ah, wonderful! Now if Carla would just leave that stupid tennis player, everything would be OK.
Rocky: I don't think that's going to happen, Joe.
(Carla enters.)
Carla: Ready to go, Rocky?
Rocky: Uh-huh.
Joe: Carla!
Carla: Joe! What a surprise!
Rocky: I think you two know each other. This is my girlfriend.
Joe: Wait a minute! If you're his girlfriend, then he's . . .
Rocky: That's right, Joe. I'm the stupid tennis player!